CHILDREN DISCOVER READING

An Introduction to Structural Reading

CHILDREN

DISCOVER

READING

An Introduction to

Structural Reading

by Catherine Stern

& Toni S. Gould

RANDOM HOUSE / L. W. SINGER COMPANY

TO *Fred, Tim, Jeff, Katherine, and Kathy*

Preface

Structural Reading is a systematic method of teaching children to read. It does so by giving them insight into the relationship between the spoken language and its written counterpart. The children are given tools that enable them, by means of the independent use of their minds, to develop the ability to read, write, and spell. Structural Reading is analogous to Structural Arithmetic in its approach to the process of learning, imparting insight into the structure of the subject matter to be mastered.

We call this method Structural Reading because of its emphasis on understanding *structure*. In learning to read, the structural characteristics to be grasped differ from step to step according to the task at hand. The Structural Reading course begins with an analysis of the *spoken word* and proceeds, step by step, in a systematic progression, to give the child insight into the structure of the *written* word—the sentence, the paragraph, the story. Learning by insight enables the child to transfer what he has already grasped to the understanding of new tasks. In this method, to learn means to discover and explore, never to memorize by rote.

To teach reading means to introduce the child to the written form of the English language. In teaching Structural Reading we do not study the language as such; this is the province of the linguist. Rather, we build on what the child already knows, the spoken language. We begin by making the child aware of initial sounds; he hears them as he pronounces words and then learns how these sounds are transcribed by letters. Subsequently he learns to take spoken words apart and to put them together again, discovering while he does so how the words he has analyzed are recorded. The written word is thus immediately identified with the familiar spoken word, and the child never loses his grasp of its meaning; the written word talks back to him, so to speak, so that he realizes that writing is simply a way to fix speech on a page.

We emphasize the teaching of sounds and we rely on sounding words out, but we do not turn the clock back to outmoded phonics instruction. Instead of starting with the study of disparate, meaningless letters and the piecemeal blending of the sounds they represent, Structural Reading follows a new course. Our children start by sounding out each word—analyzing each spoken and printed word into its component parts; since the children know what they are doing, they can proceed confidently, each at his own rate, to the recognition of the studied words "at sight."

Reading at sight is the goal of the method, not its beginning. The children learn to *read* exactly what is printed on the page; they do not need a host of clues for word identification. Structural analysis forms the center of every lesson throughout the Structural Reading course. Whereas in other methods structural analysis is only one of the clues for identifying the printed word, in this method it is applied consistently at every level. From the very first decoding of a word to the eventual study of the function of the magic *e* or the workings of an intricate spelling rule, children are taught to analyze structural characteristics.

This method has been set forth in five combination workbook readers which we wrote with Margaret B. Stern and Marion Gartler as our co-authors:

BOOK	TITLE	LEVEL
A (Readiness)	*We Learn to Listen*	Kindergarten
B	*We Discover Reading*	1a
C	*We Read and Write*	1b
D	*We Read More and More*	2a
E	*Now We Read Everything*	2b

These worktexts, aimed primarily at children in kindergarten through the end of the second grade, constitute a complete program for teaching reading, writing, spelling, and even elementary grammar. They form the Structural Reading Series published by The L. W. Singer Company, Inc., in 1963.*

Every step of the Structural Reading method originated in actual teaching and was tested and improved in teaching situations. Our experience includes teaching five-year-olds how to read *before* going to school as well as remedial work with older children who had failed to learn to read in school. In observing our five-year-olds, we could study the entire process of learning to read, as it were, in slow motion. We recorded the comments our students made in the course of their lessons and illustrative excerpts are presented throughout the book. Over the years we wrote down our teaching procedures and finally condensed them into worktexts. These, too, were tested and retested in teaching both individual children and large school classes. Changes suggested by these teaching experiences were incorporated in the final, published form of the worktexts.

The Structural Reading Method has been and is currently being used on an experimental basis in various public schools. Mrs. Dorothy Whittington tried out the method with children, whose IQ's ranged from average to low, in a public school in a culturally deprived area of Seattle. She found that Structural Reading enabled her to get much better results with her classes than she had ever achieved with other teaching methods in previous years. When the worktexts were published, in March 1963, several pilot projects were launched. The method is now being used in more than ten New York City public schools, where the children come from culturally deprived backgrounds. These children had no preschool activities as a preparation for reading.

With the first year of teaching these classes completed, it is evident to teachers, parents, and visitors that the children do not only know how to read but that they eagerly try to read any book at their level of interest. Parents report that this happy absorption in reading also continues at home. Preliminary test

* Most of the teaching aids and games which we describe in this book—Key Picture Cards for classroom use, the *Picture Dictionary*, Picture Lotto sets with cards, cardboard dominoes, and supplementary reading booklets to accompany Books B and C—are also available from the L. W. Singer Company, Inc., 249 West Erie Boulevard, Syracuse 2, New York. Many of the games described are to be found in the teacher's editions of the Structural Reading Series worktexts.

results and the detailed evaluations of observing educators describing the children's success in reading are quoted in Chapter 12.

Throughout the book we have used the comments of the individually taught children, comments that show interest, joy, and success in reading.

This book is designed primarily for teachers who want to teach reading by the Structural Reading Method and for college students who are studying methods of teaching reading. We hope, though, that it will also interest educators, psychologists, and parents. It should be of special interest to those who have been looking for a method by which almost all children can learn to read with enjoyment and efficacy.

Acknowledgments

This book is dedicated to those members of our family who learned to read by this method and whose comments greatly contributed to this book.

The French call the midwife *sage femme,* and we were fortunate to have had three wise women to help us bring this book into the world. We want to express our thanks to Deborah C. Roberts, who edited an early and incomplete draft of the book. We are greatly indebted to Jane Schilling, who went through the manuscript page by page and whose innumerable suggestions and penetrating criticism improved the text greatly. We are very grateful to Beatrice K. Hofstadter who put her masterly editorial touch on the finished manuscript.

We appreciate the pioneering work of Dorothy Whittington, the first teacher to try out the method in her public school class in Seattle, Washington, and of Marion Gartler, co-author of the Structural Reading series. Our deepest gratitude goes to Dr. Charles M. Shapp, Assistant Superintendent of school districts 12, 13, and 14 of the City of New York, who had the fortitude to introduce the method as a pilot project in six public school classes. In his determination to help children in deprived areas to learn to read better, he encouraged the experimenting with a new method. We are equally indebted to Mrs. Evelyn A. Farrar, Reading Consultant to these districts, under whose expert guidance the project was initiated and conducted. We would also like to gratefully acknowledge the cooperation of Mrs. Betty Yarborough, Director of the Developmental Program, Chesapeake

Public Schools, Chesapeake, Virginia, and Mrs. Evelyn Ely, Supervisor, Chesapeake Schools, where Structural Reading was also tried out.

Thanks are also due to Dr. David Gould for his many stimulating suggestions and for his help in evaluating the test results. We are particularly pleased that Mr. Edward B. Gasser was kind enough to put our preliminary test results into a computer to obtain the statistical data published in this book. Finally, we are especially grateful to our traditional collaborator, Margaret B. Stern, who helped in many ways, not the least of which was by keeping other work from interrupting us.

Contents

Preface   vii

PART ONE   CRITICAL EVALUATION OF
METHODS OF TEACHING READING   1

Chapter 1   Learning by Insight   3
Chapter 2   Learning to Read with the D'Rilly
              Alphabet   15
Chapter 3   Structural Reading: A New Approach   28

PART TWO   AN OUTLINE OF THE TEACHING
COURSE IN STRUCTURAL READING   39

Chapter 4   The Pre-Reading Program: From Initial
              Sounds to Letters   41
Chapter 5   From the Spoken to the Printed Word   54
Chapter 6   From Reading Words to Reading
              Sentences and Stories   69
Chapter 7   The Systematic Expansion of the Reading
              and Writing Vocabulary   90

Chapter 8 From the Spoken Word to Spelling Rules and the First Grammatical Concepts 107

Chapter 9 From the Skill of Reading to the Related Reading Skills 127

PART THREE ADJUSTING THE STRUCTURAL READING PROGRAM TO INDIVIDUALS 147

Chapter 10 Providing for Individual Growth 149

Chapter 11 Games and Other Teaching Aids 158

Chapter 12 Preliminary Test Results and Four Case Studies 178

SUMMARY 219

Index 223

PART ONE CRITICAL
EVALUATION OF METHODS
OF TEACHING READING

CHAPTER ONE

Learning by Insight

Americans believe in education as a force for human progress, and have long had the habit of affirming their faith in it both publicly and privately. Yet in recent years a suspicion seems to have grown up that most current intellectual and scientific achievements are the work of men who have triumphed over their education, rather than profited by it. This uneasiness, added to a growing awareness that children ought to read and compute better than they do and combined with other dissatisfactions about American education, has stimulated considerable public discussion and has led parents, educators, and other interested citizens to re-examine our elementary school system.

Various studies of education have suggested that there are two principal causes of the prevailing dissatisfaction: first, the average product of our schools reads no better now than his counterpart did twenty-five years ago; and second, the methods used to teach children the basic skills seem to have a tendency towards numbing rather than stimulating their minds. The truly deadly effect of methods that stifle rather than encourage creativity is being recognized more and more and is being loudly deplored. Our children must learn *to reason, to use their minds,* from the first moment they enter school. In his outstanding book on the history of progressive education, Lawrence A. Cremin insists that this is the schools' central responsibility: "By training all in the ability to think, the schools distribute intellectual power widely among the people. This and this alone is their distinctive way of contributing to social progress." [1]

In a modern first grade, children actively explore their surroundings. When, however, they begin to learn to read, their learning is all too often not discovering, but memorizing. The learning process itself has no vitality. The pupil passively listens to the teacher and repeats what she says until he can reproduce her words by himself. He rarely discovers anything about the nature of the subject. The child's rote memory is taxed to the utmost and yet his intelligence lies dormant.

For many people, learning seems to be identified with memorizing, whereas others view learning as thinking, finding solutions, discovering. For both views there are experiments in psychology that illustrate the essential points.

The view that rote memorization is the essential process in learning found its greatest support in Edward Thorndike's famous animal experiments published in 1898.

In one of these experiments a cat was placed in a cage from which it tried to escape. With frantic movements the cat tried to get free; by chance it moved the lever that opened the cage. Each time the experiment was repeated, the period of trial and error was shortened until, finally, the cat immediately jumped at the lever and escaped. The cat had *learned* to connect "lever" and "getting out." It remembered how to solve this special problem. However, this kind of learning could help the cat only in an identical situation.[2]

The animal experiments that demonstrated the other kind of learning, learning by insight, were conducted by Wolfgang Koehler with anthropoid apes and published in 1917.

In these experiments "the animals were brought into situations in which all essential conditions were actually visible, and the solution could be achieved immediately." In one of these experiments a bunch of bananas was placed outside the cage at a distance farther than the ape could reach with his outstretched arm. Clearly within the field of vision of the animal a stick was placed on the floor of the cage. Koehler describes vividly how the animal gave up trying to reach the fruit directly; "finally she lies down for good, and takes no further interest in the objective. . . . Suddenly Tschego leaps to her feet, seizes the stick, and, quite adroitly, pulls the bananas till they are within reach."[3]

In this case the solution of the problem was not found by

trial and error, nor was it a product of chance. The experimenter made it possible for the structure of the whole situation to be clear: the role of the stick in solving the problem could be understood by the animal. The animal had learned a mode of attack and further experiments showed the phenomenon of transfer; what was grasped in one situation was used in another where conditions were somewhat different.

The learning theory worked out by Max Wertheimer, the founder of Gestalt psychology, is based on this phenomenon of learning by insight, which he proved to be not only desirable but, in most cases, possible.[4] He and his followers pointed out that learning by memorizing becomes necessary only when the subject matter to be studied does not have a structure that can be understood. Fortunately there are only a few such areas. One category, for example, is the learning of proper names—cities, mountains, rivers, flowers, etc. Wertheimer showed, however, that in a subject like geometry, which has a clearcut structure, children will learn by insight if the teacher makes the structure of the subject matter visible to them. It has been proven to Wertheimer's satisfaction that this same phenomenon is to be observed when children are taught arithmetic by insight. "In many years of study with children, Dr. Catherine Stern has developed tools and methods for the teaching of arithmetic in which genuine discovery in tasks of a structural nature play an essential role. The results in learning—and in happiness—seem extraordinarily good as compared with the usual teaching by drill which focuses on forming associative bonds, etc." [5] Instead of giving children separate, disconnected facts to memorize, they can be challenged to think and to work out solutions to problems on their own. This kind of learning is far more productive than rote memorization.

Learning by insight is a process that occurs when the teacher leads her pupils to see the structure of the subject matter under study. Every subject has its own inner structure, just as a building or a bridge has a structure which may not be immediately visible but which governs its shape and stability; no structural part can be removed without destroying the whole edifice. The teacher's task is similar to that of the architect. She must view the subject matter as an integrated whole; each of its parts has its proper role to play, and none can be detached from the rest without disrupting the successful functioning of the whole. In every area the teacher must analyze the structure of a subject and put it before the pupil. The pupil will then be able to discover the structure by his own mental efforts and, while doing so, will make the subject matter his own. Under these conditions learning becomes a dynamic process in which both teacher and pupil play an active role. Not only does the child benefit from this kind of instruction, but the teacher derives great satisfaction. As Wertheimer points out, "Every good teacher enjoys teaching and learning when really sensible learning takes place: when eyes are opened, when real grasping, real understanding occurs, when the transition takes place from blindness or inaptness to orientation, understanding, mastery; and when, in the course of such happenings, mind develops." [6]

Although in this kind of instruction children do not *learn* by rote memorization, they *remember* what they have learned; they can reconstruct in their minds what they have fully grasped. No isolated facts have to be learned; principles that can be used in new and different situations are comprehended. This is the kind of teaching advocated by Jacques Barzun: "Above all, detect blind memorizing and nip it before it becomes a habit. . . . The only thing worth teaching anybody is a principle." [7]

Teaching by insight has the additional virtue of making transfer of learning possible. What has been grasped in one area can be applied to a new field. The importance of transfer has been pointed out by Jerome Bruner: "Virtually all of the evidence of the last two decades on the nature of learning and transfer has indicated that, while the original theory of formal discipline was poorly stated in terms of the training of faculties, it is indeed a fact that massive general transfer can be achieved by appropriate learning, even to the degree that learning properly under optimum conditions leads one to 'learning how to learn.' . . . These studies have stimulated a renewed interest . . . in learning designed to produce general understanding of the structure of a subject matter." [8] According to Bruner, the merits of a method of instruction in *any* subject should be judged by examining whether or not it makes the structure of the subject matter visible to the child.

Everything that has been said about teaching by insight in general holds true for the teaching and learning of reading.

The way first-, second-, and third-graders are taught to read has a direct bearing on how efficiently they will be able to use their language to read, speak, or write. To evaluate the various methods several questions must be raised. Does the reading program spur children in the independent use of their intelligence, or is the process of mastering reading skills based on drill and repetition? Does it give them insight into the structure of the spoken and written language, or are they mechanically memorizing the shape of a word or the blending of letter-sounds?

Before discussing how reading should be taught, the essential nature of the reading process must be examined. Reading is the art of extracting the meaning of a text, a meaning transmitted by written or printed characters. The accomplished reader glances at a text, and as his eyes sweep over the lines he grasps the thought expressed in the passage and reacts to it in his mind. He can often anticipate what the next sentence will say. He may be elated or depressed by the content, he may admire or deplore the ability of the writer, or he may acquire some new knowledge. He has been freed from the mechanics of reading and can grasp the meaning of the text instantly, as he would if the author were talking to him. He never consciously reads single words. As his eyes are sweeping over words, phrases, sentences, he reacts directly to the content.

The young child must be brought to the mastery of this complicated skill. Today two different methods each claim to possess the key to the best method of teaching beginners to read—the phonics approach and the sight approach. With charges and countercharges, with attacks and defenses, heated arguments rage between the two camps. Should the child be taught the letters of the alphabet first and then learn to sound out words letter by letter? Or should instruction begin with the sight of a familiar "whole word" which the pupil will learn to recognize by its shape and total configuration?

In our view, the proponents of the phonics method are right to condemn the sight method because it teaches by mechanical drill: a child must learn by considerable repetition to associate the shape of a word with the name the teacher attaches to it. The proponents of the sight method condemn the pure phonics approach, however, on exactly the same grounds—the lifeless drill required to teach the blending of separate sounds can have no natural interest for a child. Today the sight program is recognizing more and more the value of phonics but insists that phonetic analysis is meaningful only when it is applied to a whole word that a child has already learned to recognize at sight. In addition to phonic clues, picture clues and context clues are used as supplementary tools to develop word identification. The inadequacy of these aids will be discussed more fully in the next chapter.

In order to decide which is the best way of teaching a child to read the recorded form of his language, surely we must consider the characteristics of the system by which spoken language is recorded. Is it a phonetic system wherein symbols refer to the sounds of speech? Or is it a nonphonetic system, where each written word is a separate entity, a system in which a child would learn to read by memorizing several thousand ideographs?

What kind of language is English? Our system of recording language is demonstrably phonetic. That is, there is a definite relation between the sounds of speech and the letter-symbols that record them. When people say English is not a phonetic language they really mean that the phonetic system of recording English speech is erratic and unreliable.

But even though, in English, the correlation between sounds and symbols does not have a consistent, one-to-one correlation, there is nonetheless a *usable* correlation between a sound and its symbol. To abandon completely the use of this correlation because of its aberrations and to resort to memorizing each word as if it were an ideograph in a nonphonetic language seems not only unreasonable but oblivious of the very structure of the English language. It is true that the child learning to read and write English faces a harder task than the child learning to read and write Finnish or Italian, but how much easier it is than learning to read and write Chinese!

There have always been advocates for the phonetic approach.[9] This approach to the teaching of reading is based on the relationship of sound and letter. All phonetic methods begin by teaching the child the alphabet. The usual procedure is to draw the child's attention to the form of a printed letter and tell him the sound it records. Unfortunately, the association of a strange letter with a meaningless sound merely glues together two unfamiliar items; the child can only learn them by rote. Moreover, once he has learned the sounds symbolized by the letters, he must then learn to fuse these sounds: he must learn that *m* plus *a* says *ma*, plus *n* says *man*. As McKee [10] and others have pointed out, the separate sounds *m a n* pronounced consecutively do not produce the word *man*. The sounds have to be *blended* before the word can emerge. Only children with a special aptitude can sound out *j u m p* and arrive at the word *jump*. Others must be taught laboriously how to blend.

Most pupils acquire the necessary skill of blending only after protracted drilling. The mechanics of these first steps may be so difficult that no energy will be left for thinking about the meaning of the word that has just been pronounced. All too often the method produces "word callers" who can read a whole passage, word by word, but who do not know what the text says.

It cannot and must not be regarded as reading when a child merely pronounces what the sounds say without realizing the full meaning of what he reads. The act of reading, by definition, means "to observe and to apprehend the meaning of something written, printed, etc." (*The American College Dictionary*)

Not only do phonetic approaches often violate these requirements, but, as will be shown in Chapter 3, linguistic approaches disregard them also. Leonard Bloomfield's [11] teaching course, for instance, is based on word lists that include senseless phonograms among familiar words. There is no meaning to be found in artificial words like *pec* or *noc* which the child learns to pronounce correctly. It is a dangerous practice to give the child the feeling that reading is just the unthinking rendition of the sounds the letters indicate. A child must be taught from the start that reading means grasping what the author intended to convey. Whenever meaning is not seen as the vital factor in reading, the method of teaching misses the point.

In contrast to most phonetic and linguistic methods, the sight method insists on reading for meaning from the beginning of instruction. However, it is the teacher who hands the meaning of a word to the child by telling him what the word says. The child cannot decipher it by himself since he has not been taught the correspondence of letters and sounds. His task is to remember the shape of the whole word well enough to recognize it when he sees it again. When the child reads the first primer, the meaning is once more provided for him, not by the teacher but this time by pictures and the context of the story; all too often he is guessing what a word says since he has not been given the tools to decipher it. But the natural sequence is to first read a word or a sentence and then to grasp its meaning; to reverse the sequence does not make sense.

The sight method makes use of the observation that the experienced reader is not aware of letters or syllables but that he recognizes whole words, phrases, and sentences at a time. It has been found that some children can learn to read by this procedure. Some proponents of the sight method claim that their approach is based on Gestalt psychology, because the whole word, not its single letters, are taken as the point of departure. This, however, is a misinterpretation of Wertheimer's theory of teaching and learning. The salient point in Wertheimer's theory is the fact that the relationship of a meaningful whole and its parts is clearly grasped: it is the role and function of the parts in building up the whole which is the key to understanding.

The starting point in teaching reading must indeed be a meaningful whole, not a chance form such as the outward configuration of a printed or written word which cannot provide a basis for learning by insight. The black marks on the paper have not been put down by an artist to make an identifiable picture. A Chinese ideograph, which does give some pictorial clues, conveys some information about its meaning, but an English word reveals nothing about itself by its outer configuration. There is no structural relation between the *shape* of the word and the word itself. To teach reading by gluing two unrelated items together can never lead to insight.

In the sight method, reading is taught as if there were nothing to learn but the attaching of names to the shape of words. However, reading is certainly not a case of learning *names,* as with flowers, rivers, or mountains.

Reading can be learned by insight if we begin with the *spoken word* as the meaningful whole and base our study on the role and function of sounds in building whole words. As we will show, once the structure of the spoken word is grasped, the structure of the printed word will then be understood.

The sight method takes the performance of the accomplished reader as the model for the beginning of reading instruction. The method does not achieve its desired goal, and, indeed, it would be strange if it did. In every area of teaching and learning the beginning steps are qualitatively different from expert performance at the last stage, the stage of mastery. To expect a beginner to learn to read by imitating an accomplished adult is like trying to teach a baby who has yet to speak his first word to talk in sentences. Although the teaching of reading should aim at developing every single skill of the expert reader, one cannot but begin at the beginning; progress toward the goal must be made through steps which are meaningful on each successive level.

Since neither of the two familiar approaches to the teaching of reading allows for learning by insight, it would seem logical and expedient to look for a new course of instruction. An analogy taken from three possible ways of teaching botany may help to clarify what we mean.

One approach to the teaching of botany calls for the teacher and pupils to dissect a flower into separate, lifeless pieces. The children learn the names of the pieces by heart—sepals, petals, stamens, pistils—and they are instructed to remember how many of each a particular flower possesses. It would be hard, if not impossible, for a child to put the disparate pieces together again in his mind, to reconstruct the shape or beauty, least of all the fragrance, of the whole living flower. This approach resembles the old-fashioned method of teaching phonics. Senseless configurations (letters) and dissected word parts (phonograms) are studied and then must be assembled into whole words. To learn by means of such a procedure requires great effort, and many a child misses the meaning of the whole word.

In protest against the first method, a second kind of teacher brings live flowers to school and draws the children's attention to the shape, color, and fragrance of each specimen. She teaches the children the name of each flower, a name that will be associated with the separate impression each individual flower makes. She may point out at some time that flowers have sepals, petals, stamens, and pistils, but since these parts are introduced as disconnected pieces, the child cannot understand the function of each part in the life of the flower. This approach is analogous to teaching reading by the sight method. The general shape of a whole word is connected with its name, but no attention is paid to the function of the letters and their role in the structure of the word.

A third approach, which we may call Structural Botany, is described in Compton's encyclopedia: "We can enjoy a flower's beauty and perfection of form more fully if we understand its structure and how each part helps in the work of seed making. A typical flower has four sets or organs. . . . The sepals are the lower and outer-most part of the flower. They fold over the tender, closed bud and protect it from cold and other injuries while it is developing. . . . The petals attract insects and humming birds to help in the work of pollination. . . ." [12]

This approach examines not only the whole living flower but also the separate parts, pointing out their function and role in the flower's whole life. Even color and fragrance are viewed as fulfilling structural functions in the flower's life; they attract the insects which are necessary to bring the pollen from pistils to stamens.

Similarly, the teaching of reading must start with the study of the *whole spoken word,* which is already full of meaning to the beginning reader. The child must be helped to understand the function of sounds and word parts in building up each whole spoken word. Such a course of teaching would start neither with piecing together meaningless letters nor with studying the peculiar "shape" of each printed word.

There can be no doubt that both teaching by phonics and teaching by sight forces the child to learn to read by the use of rote memorization. At bottom, both approaches try to teach the same way: the teacher says, the child repeats. Such a learning situation can lead to nothing more than parroting, and no insight is imparted. Blind teaching inevitably leads to blind learning. Reading must be taught in such a way that the structure of the language is laid bare so clearly that from the start the beginning reader learns to read by insight rather than by rote memory.

It cannot be emphasized too strongly that for each child, reading is the skill upon which depends all he will learn in the future. It is of decisive importance for the beginning reader that he triumph rather than fail in his first experiences with reading. More than in any other field, early success or failure determines the child's attitude toward learning. If a child has learned to read well, he is prepared for the work he must do later on. If he has failed, he will carry with him a severe handicap. The serious dangers for children who have not learned to read are stressed by Dr. James B. Conant: "I am convinced that a common denominator among unsuccessful school children who later become dropouts and perhaps juvenile delinquents is the failure to develop reading skills. Once these pupils reach the junior high school, it may well be too late to salvage them." [13]

How we teach reading to a six-year old will not only influence his entire school career, but may also shape his whole life. If the beginning reader would learn to use his mind to acquire the necessary knowledge, there would be more good readers in the upper grades of our elementary schools and in our high schools and fewer children, having been defeated in their first efforts, would lose their natural eagerness to learn.

B I B L I O G R A P H I C A L   N O T E S

1. LAWRENCE A. CREMIN, *The Transformation of the School* (New York: Alfred A. Knopf, 1961), p. 345.

2. EDWARD L. THORNDIKE, *Animal Intelligence* (New York: The Macmillan Company, 1898), p. 12 ff. See also Thorndike, "Animal Intelligence," *The Psychological Review,* Series of Monograph Supplements, Vol. I, No. 4 (June 8, 1898).

3. WOLFGANG KOEHLER, *The Mentality of Apes* (New York: Harcourt, Brace and Company, 1925), pp. 31, 266.

4. MAX WERTHEIMER, *Productive Thinking* (New York: Harper and Brothers, 1945).

5. *Ibid.,* p. 108.

6. MAX WERTHEIMER, Foreword to G. Katona, *Organizing and Memorizing* (New York: Columbia University Press, 1940).

7. JACQUES BARZUN, *Teacher in America* (Boston: Little, Brown and Company, 1945), p. 85, p. 22.

8. JEROME S. BRUNER, *The Process of Education* (New York: Vintage Books, 1963), p. 6.

9. LEONARD BLOOMFIELD AND CLARENCE L. BARNHART, *Let's Read—A Linguistic Approach* (Detroit: Wayne State University Press, 1961). RUDOLF FLESH, *Why Johnny Can't Read and What You Can Do About It* (New York: Harper and Brothers, 1955). ANNA GILLINGHAM AND BESSIE W. STILLMANN, *Remedial Work for Reading, Spelling and Penmanship* (New York: Sackett and Wilhelms Lith. Corp., 1936). JULIE HAY AND CHARLES E. WINGO, *Reading with Phonics* (Philadelphia: J. B. Lippincott Company, 1954). ROMALDA BISHOP SPALDING, *The Writing Road to Reading* (New York: Whiteside, Inc. and William Morrow and Company, 1957). SYBIL TERMAN AND CHARLES CHILD WALCUTT, *Reading: Chaos and Cure* (New York: McGraw-Hill Book Company, Inc., 1958).

10. PAUL MCKEE, *The Teaching of Reading in the Elementary School* (Boston: Houghton Mifflin Company, 1948), p. 245.

11. BLOOMFIELD AND BARNHART, *op. cit.*

12. *Compton's Encyclopedia,* Vol. 5 (Chicago: F. E. Compton Co., 1958), p. 216.

13. JAMES B. CONANT, *Slums and Suburbs* (New York: The New American Library, 1964), p. 52.

CHAPTER TWO

Learning to Read with the D'Rilly Alphabet

In order to appreciate the difficulties of learning how to read, you, an adult, must look at the task as nearly as possible with the eyes of an untaught child. You need to discover for yourself the complexity of wresting words familiar to your ear and tongue and mind from their unfamiliar symbolic representation on a printed page. To enable you to have this experience, we will use a fictitious alphabet that will be as strange to you as is the English alphabet to the young beginning reader. This alphabet has been invented by one of the authors to prove that current methods of teaching reading are really based on *drill;* therefore we call it the D'Rilly alphabet.

We will substitute the D'Rilly symbols for English letters to bring out the difficulties children face in learning to read by the sight method. Let us begin with an actual first-grade class who, during a tour of their school building, came upon two large

Fig. 2.1

signs (Fig. 2.1) which they examined with interest. Back in the classroom, they discussed with their teacher what these notices had said. It was agreed that the cafetéria sign had said "Hot Lunch," and, after some debate, that the other one must have said "Wet Paint," since it was on the railing of a freshly painted stair; the teacher then wrote "hot lunch" and "wet paint" on the blackboard. Fig. 2.1 shows how these signs would look, written in D'Rilly symbols.*

An animated discussion of where members of the class had seen similar signs now followed, in which the teacher continually called the class's attention to the words written on the board, until, by the end of the morning, all of the children seemed to have learned to read both signs. Later in the day, however, another teacher, unobserved by the children, reversed the position of the signs. When she asked a little boy which sign told what the class had had to eat, he unhesitatingly pointed to the sign reproduced in Fig. 2.2.

∇∩◊ l◢ð∠◊

Fig. 2.2

Perhaps, if you had noted a distinctive initial or terminal letter, you would have seen at once that this could not be the "hot lunch" sign, but a less observant adult, like the little boy, might easily have thought that the cafeteria had served "wet paint."

In most schools where reading is taught by the sight method, similar experiences are a regular part of the learning process for first-grade children. After they have had an interesting experience such as a trip or a party, they dictate short sentences about the event to their teacher, who then writes what they

---

* The D'Rilly alphabet was created by Catherine Stern, who also invented numerical symbols used in *Children Discover Arithmetic* [1] to point out the shortcomings of the kind of arithmetic teaching that depends primarily upon rote memorization and drill.

McKee in his outstanding book *The Teaching of Reading in the Elementary Schools* [2] uses an alphabet of his own invention to explain the processes involved in reading and the teaching of reading.

have said on the board. These words are read and reread, discussed, recorded in a class album of "experience charts," and copied when the children become able to do this. Such an "experience chart," in the D'Rilly alphabet, is shown in Fig. 2.3.

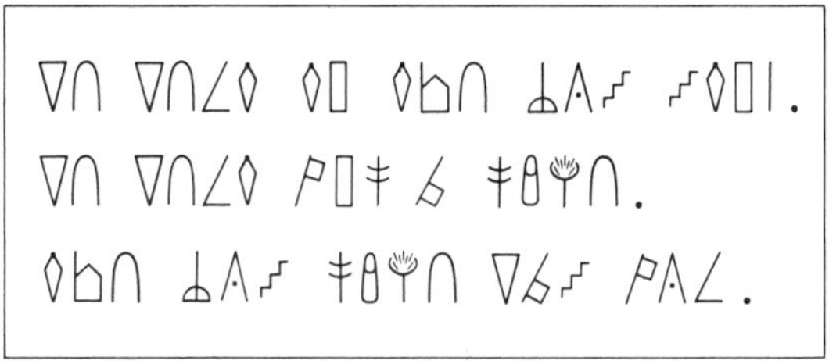

Fig. 2.3

The words say: "We went to the bus stop. We went for a ride. The bus ride was fun."

Study the word *stop:*

Study the word *ride:*

Each of these words has its particular whole word form and its characteristic ups and downs. Study the shape of each word carefully. Are you sure that you could now recognize these words in different sentences? How would you begin to figure them out if you were not sure of them?

Experience charts are supposed to provide motivation for learning to read words at sight. Their use is based on the assumption that the vivid interest a child had in the actual experience will carry over to his interest in learning the words by which the events were recorded. It is our belief that interest should be evoked by the reading experience alone, in the pleasure of deciphering words; although experience charts do have a place in the course of teaching, they should be used not to teach a child to read, but only after he has learned to read.

In the preprimers and primers used in most schools, children are presented with a limited number of words. These words are repeated many times, always in the context of illustrations that make their meaning clear. Most children have no trouble learning a word such as *Alice,* once they have associated it with the picture of a particular little girl. They pore over the page on which it first appears and soon know that

$$\measuredangle \varepsilon \theta \mathbb{C} \cap$$

must say "Alice." Seeing on the next page a mother beckoning to the same little girl, they feel sure that the text reads:

$$\measuredangle \varepsilon \theta \mathbb{C} \cap, \mathbb{C} \square \measuredangle \cap$$

or "Alice, come!" After repeatedly finding and identifying these same words on subsequent pages, most children (and you) will indeed be able to read

$$\measuredangle \varepsilon \theta \mathbb{C} \cap, \mathbb{C} \square \measuredangle \cap$$

at sight. But almost a hundred words must be learned in this laborious way before a child has acquired a basic sight vocabulary. Truly, it is amazing how many children taught by the sight method do learn to read, and equally, it is easy to understand why a great many, having tried hard, finally give way to despair.

What is worse, the sight approach may cause unnecessary difficulties for a child even before he actually begins to learn to read. Reading readiness tests usually determine how children are to be grouped within a beginners' class. Frequently, such tests contain one word written in front of a box which contains that word along with many others. The child has to single out the required word from the group in the box. Try the test yourself with words written in D'Rilly letters. Since the D'Rilly letters are easier to remember than English letters, make the test harder by covering up the word outside the box after you have looked at it. Then, from memory, try to find the same word in the box. (See Fig. 2.4.)

Whatever your difficulties with this test may be, those of a

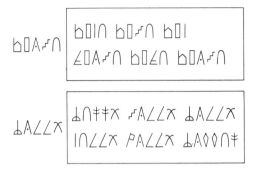

Fig. 2.4

child working with English letters will be greater. Many English letters resemble each other closely; the shapes of *b* and *d*, *f* and *t*, *p*, and *q* are so similar that it is hard for a child to see any differences between them.

It ought to be clear by now that learning to read in this way is a laborious task at best. Since no consistent mode of attack has been provided, piecemeal learning results. You may have memorized ten words and now know them by sight, but there was nothing in the process of learning the ten that will enable you to decipher an eleventh unknown word by yourself.

So haphazard an approach places a painful burden on a child's rote memory. If, for example, a child is asked to learn the two words

ხ◻∠∩   ხ◻∧ʳ∩

(*home* and *house*, respectively) by their outward appearance, he too often forgets which is which; they look very much alike and either word usually fits the same context. Understandably enough, many a child faced with such difficulties becomes discouraged.

Since the protagonists of the sight method have become aware of how hard it is to remember what a printed word means, they now advocate giving additional clues. One such word-recognition clue draws the beginner's attention to characteristics of the shape of a word. A teacher will ask children to note the "length, height, interesting up-and-down appearance" of some words like *elephant* and *happy;* the aim is to achieve identification by configuration.[3] A teacher introducing the word *monkey* is encouraged to fix the word in her pupils' memories by pointing out that the last letter of *monkey* has a tail! The inadequacy of such recognition clues is shown when the class sees words such as *money* and *candy,* which have the same "tail" at the end.

Another kind of clue to word identification that has been stressed recently is the phonic clue. The child's attention is directed to initial consonants, to significant word endings, to phonograms, or to short familiar words hidden in long ones. These phonetic clues are handed out piecemeal as crutches to help rote memory. They do not constitute a systematic phonetic attack, and therefore do not enable a child to sound out words according to their structure. The usual system of using phonetic clues does not teach children to look at the main part of a word. In reading *cat* and *hat* he is taught to recognize the "at" first and add the initial sounds last. No wonder the child attacks an unknown word by looking at the middle or the end first, instead of starting at the beginning. That the results are often disastrous is shown in tests. Arthur I. Gates mentions cases in which the "order of parts" is read incorrectly, such as *arnely* for *nearly, aws* for *saw, are* for *ear.*[4] Such reversals are the natural outcome of teaching the child to look either at the end or at the middle of the word first instead of insisting from the start on the correct left-right direction.

A third kind of clue for word identification has been called structural analysis. A child's attention is directed to prefixes and suffixes, or inflectional endings, etc., of words. In contrast to Structural Reading, however, structural analysis is not used consistently. It is lacking in the very beginning of learning, which is where it is vitally needed, and it does not help children analyze the spoken word and its printed counterpart.

A fourth aid to word recognition, supplementing the sight method, is the use of picture clues. Asked to read, "See, see, see!" under a picture of a just-opened parcel, most children quickly learn to do so, and can also recognize the same words elsewhere in an equally simple context. Upon being introduced to the expanded vocabularies of the primers, however, a number of children become distressed and confused. Should they read *house* or *home, Nancy* or *Nan, Dad* or *man?* Here, pictures cannot help them decide. In each case both words fit the picture and the context equally well. A child really dependent upon such clues finds it very difficult to read a sequence of sentences for which only one picture is given. He is forced to guess, and says any word that seems to fit. But guessing is the worst enemy of precise and thoughtful reading.

In the sight method context clues are also used to help word recognition, not only at the beginning but also when a child has progressed to reading stories. If a child is unable to read a word, he is encouraged to guess what it may say from the context. This practice violates the obvious principle that every single word helps to create the meaning of the sentence and must be figured out accurately. If a child reads, "The children played in the yard. After some time they felt _____ and went back into the house" and must guess what the word he cannot read says, he may be right or wrong, but he has no way of knowing. The reason for going back into the house may be that the children felt tired, or bored, or hungry, or cold. The very essence of good reading is to take into account every word written by the author. Real reading demands accuracy. The word a child can't read because he does not recognize its shape may well be the most important in the sentence, and a wrong guess will lead the reader astray. The effects of guessing prove so disastrous in the later grades that it is harmful to encourage it in early grades. By the time a child reaches the fifth grade, guessing hinders his progress in subjects where precise reading is needed. One of our remedial reading students (a very bright boy) read *basket* of potatoes for *bushel* in an arithmetic problem where the solution required that bushels be changed to pecks. The same habit of guessing that caused him to read *Mom* for *Mother, of* for *for* or *as* for *has* in the first grade handicapped him in mathematics as well as in reading itself. Another remedial student, a fifth-grader and also a bright child, read *big spoon* for *limestone* and consequently was hindered in his understanding of the process of making steel. The fifth grade is too late in a child's school career for him to have to begin learning to read by insight; his bad reading habits have become entrenched, his curriculum is too full to allow the time needed, and, most serious of all, his mind has been conditioned to memorize, or to despair of memorizing, rather than to understand.

Yet the majority of children do learn to read, in spite of such haphazard approaches. Nevertheless, the sight method has proven disastrous for those boys and girls who may have good minds but who lack photographic memories and therefore are poor at rote memorization. These children cannot learn even the first twenty or thirty words at sight. Since they cannot readily identify a previously learned word at a glance, they must stop at every unfamiliar word in a text and try to use phonic or other clues; again and again they will be interrupted in getting at the meaning of a sentence. After endless efforts and failures, such children, if they are lucky, are sent to remedial specialists, who try to help them with easier materials, intensive instruction in phonics, and a good dose of encouragement. But it takes a long time for even the most experienced remedial reading teacher to cure a child of the effects of failure. The worst of it is that probably a majority of these struggling children who hate reading were, when they began, not only as eager but as able to learn as any of their peers.

The sight method severely handicaps *all* children in writing and spelling even more than in reading. It is hard to avoid spelling mistakes if a child's first training has been to read through the recognition of whole words. Most young children who can recognize a word at sight cannot reproduce it correctly on paper until they have been taught to do so by a separate process. Reading a printed word at sight is one process; writing a word that one thinks of or hears is another. Overwhelming evidence that sight-reading does not carry over to spelling has necessitated that spelling be taught separately and by a different method. Spelling is most commonly taught by saying words aloud, letter by letter, from memory. If the teacher says, "slide," the pupil has to respond with *"es el i de e."* What a waste this is, not only of children's time, but of their ability to think. Memorization of the appearance of each single word and then of its sequence of letters does not provide a child with a mode of attack that will make transfer of learning possible.

Having used the D'Rilly alphabet to demonstrate the inadequacy of teaching reading by the sight method, we shall now use it to prove that if teaching starts with the analysis of the familiar *spoken word* as it is built up by sounds, reading strange symbols can be learned without great effort.

To make the learning process with the D'Rilly symbols intelligible from the start, Fig. 2.5 shows how each D'Rilly letter represents an object pictorially. Study each D'Rilly letter, say its name, and listen to the initial sound. The first letter shows an ax. Say "ax" and remember that ⚬ represents the sound [a]. Looking at the second picture, say "bell," and remember that ⚬ stands for the sound [b]. (Throughout the text a letter in brackets [ ] refers to the sound of the letter. A letter in italics—*b*—refers to the written letter which, however, in this method, is called by its sound name—[b]—not its alphabet name—bē).

THE D'RILLY ALPHABET

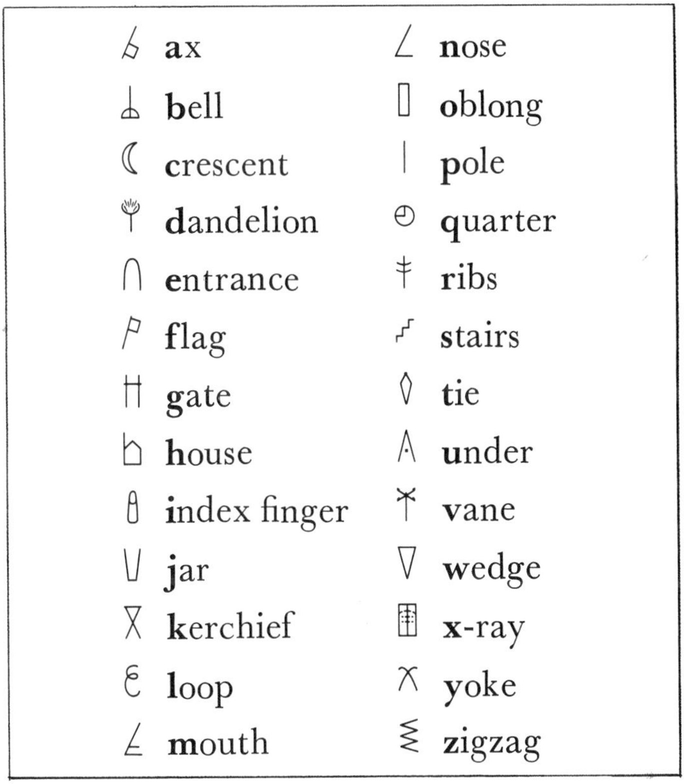

⚬	ax	∠	nose
⚬	bell	◻	oblong
☾	crescent	∣	pole
⚘	dandelion	☉	quarter
∩	entrance	‡	ribs
ᛈ	flag	ᶠ	stairs
╫	gate	◊	tie
ᗡ	house	∧	under
θ	index finger	⋏	vane
∨	jar	∇	wedge
⋈	kerchief	⊞	x-ray
Ɛ	loop	⋏	yoke
∠	mouth	⩾	zigzag

Fig. 2.5

Although after studying this alphabet you, an adult reader, can now read a word such as

◊‡θ|

by replacing the letters with their sounds, a child could not. To give a child insight into the process of reading, we must start with a *spoken word* and compare its structure to the structure of a printed word.

Look at the picture of the cat in Fig. 2.6, listen to yourself as you say "ca t" and study how the D'Rilly letters beneath the picture record the spoken sounds of *ca t*. Go on, naming each picture, then studying its written representation in the D'Rilly alphabet.

The first picture is that of a *cat*. If you break up the spoken word "cat," it falls naturally into two parts, [ca] and [t]. Therefore it makes sense that the symbols underneath the picture

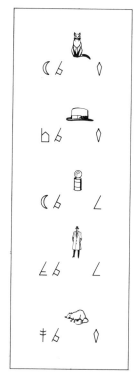

Fig. 2.6

say [ca] and [t]. The next picture shows a *hat*. You now anticipate that the written word will be broken into the component
parts [ha] and [t]. The next picture is that of a *can;* you look
at the symbols and are pleased to find that you understand them.
Next comes a picture of a *man,* and the symbols say "man" to
you. The last picture shows a *rat,* and here too, the symbols say
"rat" in an understandable way.

If you wish to learn to write these words with the D'Rilly
symbols, you will not find it very difficult. The letters are easily
reconstructed and the spelling of words in this chart is self-
evident. Without going into any further detail, it should be
clear that with such an approach, spelling does not have to be
taught separately. The structural analysis of the word *cat* discloses both how to read the word and how to write it.

You have grasped that

$$\mathbb{C}\text{\textit{b}}$$

says [ca]. This understanding helps you not only to write and
read the word

$$\mathbb{C}\text{\textit{b}}\text{\textit{0}}$$

but also to decipher the words

$$\mathbb{C}\text{\textit{b}}\,|\ \text{and}\ \mathbb{C}\text{\textit{b}}\text{\textit{∠}}\,|$$

which you have not studied. You can see from these examples
that such a teaching procedure dispenses with the learning of
one separate word after another; whole groups of words become
easy to read with confidence.

As an experienced adult reader, you know how to extract the
meaning of a whole sentence but, as we shall show later on, this
is a new step for a child. You will probably find it easy, despite
the shortness of your acquaintance with the D'Rilly alphabet,
to master the next step in the beginning process of learning to
read, which is to read whole sentences with full comprehension
(see Fig. 2.7).

These exercises will undoubtedly have taught you to read
with the D'Rilly symbols without guessing or confusion. You
would soon be able to read an entire story in D'Rilly. Here you

Fig. 2.7

have seen a clearcut, efficient way to teach reading to beginners demonstrated.

The effort of learning to read with the D'Rilly letters was undertaken by you, an adult reader, for the sake of this experiment, and not, of course, for the pleasure of reading books written in D'Rilly. For every normal child who has a strong motivation to learn to read, however, the situation is different. He has a natural curiosity and he is bent on exploring the world around him. His main activities are listening and talking, and he is eager to carry both into the interesting new field where they are called *reading* and *writing*. How fascinating to be able to have a book tell a story and to be able to tell your own story in writing so that others may read it! Most children are delighted by the prospect of learning to read, yet when they first get to school their interest is diverted; they have experiences *about* reading but no experience with the actual reading process itself, which, they are led to believe, consists of memorizing the shape of words. It is as hard for them to learn word shapes as it was for you to remember by rote that the D'Rilly word

ɾЄθ𝖸∩

says "slide."

Such a learning process is extremely dull. Since a child is only able to remember a certain number of words at sight, his sight-reading vocabulary is very limited. Accordingly, pre-primers and primers suffer from a dearth of words that can be used. Moreover, since learning to sight-read demands repetition, the same words have to be repeated endlessly in the stories to establish word recognition.

Thus, the kind of material that primers offer to keen young-sters is often appallingly simple-minded. First books say, for example, that "Mary went up, up, up," and that "Harry went down, down, down," maybe on the slide, maybe on a hill. Or children ride, ride, ride through a great many pages since they can do so on a bus, wagon, boat, or car. While the information that is being repeated in this way may fix in children's minds the outward appearance of words forming the grade-one vocabulary, it is not the stuff to make them grow.

It should not be necessary to provide extraneous interest for a child: his interest can and must be caught by the learning process itself. Many an adult reader will have deciphered the D'Rilly language with zest, enjoying the task. Almost without exception, children have equal enthusiasm for learning and, if they are taught in the right way, genuine interest will be aroused by the process of deciphering itself. This activity gives children a sense of accomplishment and a feeling of pleasure. Since it is, of course, impossible to start the teaching of reading with as exciting a story as *Tom Sawyer,* the aim must be to make the reading process itself as intriguing and delightful an adventure as possible.

BIBLIOGRAPHICAL NOTES

1. CATHERINE STERN, *Children Discover Arithmetic* (New York: Harper and Brothers, 1949).

2. PAUL MCKEE, *The Teaching of Reading in the Elementary School* (Boston: Houghton Mifflin Company, 1948).

3. ROMA GANS, *Guiding Children's Reading Through Experiences* (New York: Bureau of Publications, Teachers College, Columbia University, 1941), p. 36.

4. ARTHUR I. GATES, *Manual of Directions for Gates Reading Diagnostic Tests,* rev. ed. (New York: Bureau of Publications, Teachers College, Columbia University, 1953).

CHAPTER THREE

Structural Reading: A New Approach

The fundamental principle of Structural Reading is teaching by insight at every level of instruction.* The material taught is interesting and intelligible to the understanding of a young child. At no time is a child confronted by single, unrelated items to be blindly memorized. Instead, Structural Reading teaches children to grasp structural characteristics common to whole groups of words, and to grasp sentence structure in such a way that henceforth they can read a great many words and sentences with comprehension. As Jerome S. Bruner points out, "To learn structure, in short, is to learn how things are related." [2] Insight into structural relationships can only be gained by studying meaningful wholes, whose parts are understood in their function of building up the whole.[3]

The meaningful whole, and therefore the only meaningful point of departure, cannot be printed words, but must be *spoken words* taken from the child's speaking vocabulary, words whose meaning he already knows. Once a child has grasped the *structure* of spoken words on the oral level, he is guided to discover their counterpart in the structure of written words.

The idea of beginning with spoken language is strongly sup-

---

* In its psychology Structural Reading is analogous to *Structural Arithmetic*,[1] where we have shown that it is sensible and productive to teach arithmetic in such a way that the structural characteristics of the number system are made visible to children, who are then able to discover number facts by themselves.

ported by leading linguists.[4] Historically, speech was developed before writing was invented. In human development the young child is able to talk and to listen some years before he is ready to read. As Robert A. Hall says, "When we think of writing as more important than speech, as having a priority over speech, as determining speech, we are putting the cart before the horse in every respect: historical origin, present-day function, and present-day importance of writing with respect to speaking." [5]

Children constantly use words to describe what they have seen or to express their wishes. It is an exciting new experience to listen to a familiar word and to discover that it is composed of separable and recognizable sounds. In the Structural Reading method, children's attention is drawn first to the initial sounds that start familiar words, and then to the representation of sounds by letters. Children learn to listen to the initial sounds of words and soon discover themselves that *m*an, *m*ouse, and *m*itten all start with the same sound [m] and that *f*eather, *f*eet, and *f*ence begin with [f]. Only when sounds like [m] or [f] in their function as beginning sounds of spoken words are familiar to a child are letters introduced.

The first or Readiness Book of the Structural Reading Series, *We Learn to Listen,* teaches the correspondence between sound and letter. Each teaching page is headed by a key picture representing a familiar object. The object of the key picture is to introduce both the speech sound and the letter by which it is recorded. For instance, the child who sees the key picture of a ladder will say "ladder" to himself. He knows that the spoken word starts with the sound [l] and concludes correctly that the letter *l* which he sees as a part of the drawing must say [l]. Hence children are able to figure out for themselves that the sound [l] is represented by *l* and, conversely, that the printed letter *l* says [l].

When the sounds of all the letters have been learned, the *spoken word* is broken down into its natural parts: a child learns on the oral level how each monosyllabic word is composed of parts which he can hear separately, as when, for example, he says "ma n" or "fa n," or "ca t." The parts into which the word is broken accord with natural speech and thus seem sensible to children. When a child sees a man approaching his house, he calls to his mother, "A *ma n*!" This natural way of separating the child's spoken words is fundamental to teaching reading by insight. Learning to read in *Structural Reading* means that each child recognizes that the printed word *ma n says* [man], which is a word he knows.

This conception differs from the linguistic approach advocated by Charles C. Fries. "Learning to read, therefore, means developing a considerable range of high-speed recognition responses to specific sets of patterns of graphic shapes." [6] While this procedure may be linguistically sound, it deprives the child of the experience of learning by discovery, that is, by using his mind.

The Structural Reading course starts with phonetically regular words which have a clearcut structure; the child learns to sound out each word with full understanding. The teaching course of Structural Reading progresses from the ă words to the ĭ, ŏ, ŭ, and ĕ words. Pictures are used to elicit a familiar, spoken word.

For example, each child looks at the picture of a fan on page 3 of *We Discover Reading* (see Plate 1), says "fan," and then looks below the picture to discover how this word is recorded by letters. The child sees that the spoken main part [fa] is recorded by *fa*. He says [fa] and adds the ending [n]. This step leads to the meaningful reading of the word *fan*. The child listens to himself as he says the two parts [fa n], then a flash of insight occurs and, as one child exclaimed, "Fa n, a fan! We use it when it's very hot!" This spontaneous remark shows that this child read the word *fan* with full comprehension; at this moment the printed word acquired the meaning of the spoken word for which it stands. By this means children learn a mode of attack: by saying the names of the pictures and then analyzing the words that are recorded, they realize that each of the words falls into two parts: the main word-part, pronounced as a unit, and the final consonant which is added to complete the word. (*Fa-n, ma-t, ca-p.*) Thus the main word-part is given to him as a ready-made blend. This is a significant departure from the typical phonetic approach, where the child has to learn that [f] + [a] says [fa], a difficult procedure at best. This piecemeal blending constituted the major flaw in previous approaches.

The most interesting part of teaching with this method is observing how pupils think. A child will work hard to decipher each word since the picture that accompanies it may be ambiguous. The picture may have been drawn to illustrate a fish or its fin, but the printed word discloses what is meant.

Peter (age 5;0) * studied a picture of a man with a hat in the work-text and guessed that the word below said "hat." Asked to sound the word out, he read: "Ma n, man! They mean the man and not the hat." Then he turned to the teacher and said: "You know, pictures sometimes fool you but words really don't."

A child taught by the Structural Reading method realizes from the start that he must read no word but the right one. Confidence is born only from such complete understanding. It is the teacher's job to show a beginning reader that each written word, just as each spoken word, conveys a specific meaning he must *know*. We cannot stress often enough the basic importance to a child's development, not only as a reader but also as a thinker, of realizing from the very first that only *knowing* will do. It is impossible for a child to arrive at actual reading until he has learned first, that he must know what the word says, and second, that he must know what it means.

When children learn to read through insight into the structure of words, they are given the key to reading words they have not studied. Our records, many of which we present in the following parts of this book, show an overwhelming amount of such transfer. Children who have understood the structure of the word *man* are equipped to read the words *sad* and *mad* unaided. Many children who studied the first page of *t*-words carefully read the next two pages right off.

Transfer or carry-over occurs consistently, not only from the words studied to the entire group of structurally related words, but also to unrelated new words. When a child has been taught a *mode of attack,* rather than a list of unrelated sight words, he is able to decipher similar words without any further teaching help.

Jeff (6;5) gave his mother the following account of an experience he had at the beginning of first grade. "Mom, there was a word in our book, and every child in class said, 'It says pretty.' I had never read the word but I saw it didn't have a 'pr,' so I knew it couldn't

---

* A figure such as 5;0 gives the age of the child whose name it follows. It means 5 years, 0 months old.

say 'pretty.' It started with 'par' and ended with 'ty,' so I knew it was *party*. I was right. How can you say pretty when you see there is no *pr?*"

While it is essential that each pupil acquire the tools to enable him to decipher words himself, he must learn to leave the tools behind when he no longer needs them. After a child has been taught how to sound out single words, he must then be helped to recognize these words instantly, without sounding out. A glance at a word must suffice to convey its meaning. Fluent reading depends on instant recognition and interpretation. Thus, though beginning instruction in Structural Reading is decidedly different from that used in the sight method, the two methods have the same goal. In Structural Reading, however, reading by sight becomes a short-cut which the child comes to naturally, after he has understood what he is doing.

How is this momentous step achieved? Certainly not by directing children to study the outward appearance of words. Progressing from the more or less slow deciphering of a word to its instant recognition requires nothing more than practice. Without any specific help from their teachers, children one day discover with delight that a glance is enough to identify a printed word that formerly had to be deciphered by sounding out.

The process involved is analogous to the way a pianist learns to play a melody in one swift and coherent movement. A beginning student learns the correspondence between the printed notes and the keys of the piano; this enables him to strike separate tones, note by note. It is understanding of structure, and then continued practice, that brings him to the point at which, when his eyes are moving over the notes, his fingers unconsciously follow on the keys. Only then can he play with expression and correct rhythm.

Somewhat the same thing happens when a newcomer must learn to find his way around a strange city. The best way to orient himself is by studying a map that shows the structure of the section through which he is to walk. The first day he clings to the map for help, reads every street sign, and checks every turn. After only a few trips made with hesitant steps he can walk to his destination with assurance. Now, without any conscious effort, his eyes notice a shop at a corner where he should turn, or a traffic light where he must cross a street.

In both of these instances, it is practice that transforms the halting steps of a beginner into the confident performance of an expert. In the same way, it is practice that leads a beginning reader from the careful sounding out of words to recognizing them at sight.

Reading single words at sight must precede reading simple sentences. To grasp the meaning of a whole sentence is a *new* step in the process of learning to read, and is considerably more difficult than grasping the meaning of one word.

A pupil might know many Latin words but be helpless if asked to translate a written sentence. Reading a sentence word by word is not enough. The meaning of a sentence is *not* derived from a piecemeal addition of the single words contained in it. Some words are manifestly more important than others. To seize the thought of a sentence, one must determine intellectually the relationships of each single word to every other; in many ways this is similar to constructing a word phonetically from its components. A child has to be taught that every sentence is a whole thought; he must learn to analyze the role each single word plays in the sentence structure. Later on, he must learn that each sentence plays a definite role in a paragraph or a story. Again, the task is not accomplished by reading one sentence after another in piecemeal fashion. The reader must learn to extract the thought from the text as a whole. The initial stage of reading centers on single words, but the final stage is not reached until complex material can be read comprehendingly and critically.

In the Structural Reading course, reading and writing are taught together, because this is their natural relationship. Reading and writing not only spring from the same source, but nothing is more helpful in reading words than constructing them as is done in writing. Writing is the natural counterpart of reading; they are complementary language aspects and so must be taught together.

The monosyllabic words with which the course begins lend themselves as well to writing as to reading, since the sounds and letters correspond so closely. As soon as a child knows how to translate sounds into letters, he will not make spelling mistakes. He does not, for example, have to spell out *man* as *em ay en*; rather, he listens to himself pronounce the word [ma n] and then writes the main word part and the ending. He has learned how to record sounds by written symbols. This method, in fact, reproduces how written language was derived from speech.

To begin by sounding out monosyllabic words accords with the concepts of leading linguists; the late Leonard Bloomfield wrote, "We can best help him by giving him the most suitable words to read, and these are short words in which the letters have uniform values. We present as many as possible of these, without regard to their meanings. The child will get the meanings only when he has solved the mechanical problems of reading. . . . When the *an* group has been learned, we may go on to another final-group, such as bat, fat, hat, mat, Nat, pat, rat, sat, tat, vat." [7]

Our teaching experiences have confirmed the validity of Bloomfield's ideas about the kind of words with which study should begin, but we do not agree that meaningless, artificially made-up words should be taught. To provide practice of the blending process Bloomfield's followers present nonsense syllables, such as "tat, jan, yip, wen, fen, . . ." [8] In Structural Reading we insist on comprehension from the start; only meaningful words, which children have heard many times before and which, after sounding out, can be easily understood, can teach children to comprehend what they are reading. A child who has sounded out the word *man,* can also explain what the word means.

Understanding the meaning of the words a child reads is of the utmost importance; the expression "reading for meaning" is, indeed, a tautology. If the meaning of a word or sentence is not grasped, *no reading has taken place.* A child who has been taught by the Structural Reading method knows he has not read a word correctly until its meaning is clear to him.

Kathy (6;0) tried to decipher the impressive words on the title page of a dictionary. She carefully sounded out the word "collegiate," pronouncing it in a fair approximation. Then she remarked: "I figured it out but I did not read it really. I do not know what it means."

Another major difference between Bloomfield's method and Structural Reading is concerned with the grouping of the words to be studied. We do not lump together words that have the same final-groups of letters. We do not teach that *c + an* says *can.*

Since [c] + [an] are not readily pronounced as [can], the blend can be learned only by drill. In speaking we break the word [can] naturally into [ca] and [n]. The [c] is welded to the vowel, and therefore the structure of the word requires that it break into [ca] [n] not [c] [an]. Further, when the *an* or *at* family is taught as a group, attention is directed first to the *end* of the words studied. Since English reading or writing proceeds in one direction only, from left to right, it is wrong to emphasize an ending as a clue to a word. Just as the child who is learning to count must be taught to say 1 2 3 and not 2 3 1, the proper sequence of sounds and letters must be strictly adhered to, in order to avoid confusion. A six-year-old knows better than to put on his shoes before his socks. It must become equally natural with him to start with first things first in reading and writing, and to follow the correct sequence from left to right without hesitation.

There is yet another reason why we do not group words according to the phonograms that form their endings. We have found that it is far more productive of further learning to teach children word-beginnings. A child who discovers that *can, cat,* and *camp* all start with the same main word-part [ca] will attack more complex words such as *calendar* or *camel* with confidence because he is sure about the beginning. Structural Reading thus equips children with a tool to unlock a multitude of words.

From the monosyllabic words in which each sound is uniformly recorded by one and only one letter, children must eventually advance to the study of phonetically irregular words. In Structural Reading the analysis of these words follows the same principle underlying the study of phonetically regular words. Here again, we develop insight into the structure of the word. The spoken word [coat], for instance, has its main part and its ending; children have only to learn that the sound of the long *o* is recorded in this word by the two letters *o* and *a*. A group of such words is taught together. We have carefully assembled irregular words in related groups—groups with silent letters, with more than two syllables, and so on—because we have found that such grouping makes for confident progress in word identification. By the end of the second grade, books without a controlled vocabulary are accessible to children taught by this method.

As the successive steps in the course of teaching are described in the following chapters, it will be seen that the Structural Reading program provides the kind of systematic and complete language arts program that has been demanded by Emmet A. Betts,[9] Arthur I. Gates,[10] William S. Gray,[11] David H. Russell,[12] Paul A. Witty,[13] and many others. The course begins with an analysis of the spoken word and ends with the development of related reading skills. Once the mechanics of reading are mastered, the goal of reading instruction changes; reading becomes a means for acquiring knowledge and for recreation.

To assure achievement of these ultimate goals, and to avoid the risk of failure, beginning reading must give children a secure foundation of knowledge. Structural Reading is carefully planned to teach children to master the reading process with growing insight and competence. The study of spoken words is the only means by which children can begin to learn by insight. As soon as a child who has studied the structure of spoken words opens his worktext, he will discover reading by himself.

Since he has learned by insight into structural characteristics, two important phenomena can be observed: reconstruction and transfer. Although we have found in our practical teaching experiences an almost 100 percent retention of known words with the children taught by this method, the children are not lost even if they do not recognize at a glance a word that they read at sight before summer vacation. Since they have a secure mode of attack, they can reconstruct the word by sounding it out, and soon it will belong again to their sight vocabulary.

The occurrence of transfer widens the child's reading vocabulary. The child is able to apply what he knows to each successively more difficult task, and his vocabulary soon surpasses that of any basal reader series. The latter program, according to an estimate of Edward William Dolch,[14] expects that between 200 and 300 words will be learned by the end of the first grade. With this limited vocabulary the child learns to read just one reading series; he is not equipped to read books of another series with a different word list. The Structural Reading method gives children command over 750 words by the end of the first grade—words that they can read at a glance, write, and spell. Actually, since they have been taught to analyze the structure of words, they have many more words within their reach;

indeed, they can decipher all the words related to the ones they have studied. Equipped with so rich and extensive a vocabulary, a child at the end of the first grade will be able to read a great variety of books suitable to his age and interests.

The basic tenet of the course of Structural Reading, then, is that every step in the process be intelligible, and both thinking and reasoning are developed from the start. From the learning process itself each child acquires a feeling of adequacy and self-reliance; he owes his success to his own efforts and his own discoveries, to the power of his own mind.

BIBLIOGRAPHICAL NOTES

1. CATHERINE STERN, *Children Discover Arithmetic* (New York: Harper and Brothers, 1949).

2. JEROME S. BRUNER, *The Process of Education* (New York: Vintage Books, 1963), p. 7.

3. MAX WERTHEIMER, *Productive Thinking* (New York: Harper and Brothers, 1945).

4. LEONARD BLOOMFIELD AND CLARENCE L. BARNHART, *Let's Read—A Linguistic Approach* (Detroit: Wayne State University Press, 1961). ROBERT A. HALL, *Linguistics and Your Language* (New York: Doubleday & Company, 1960). CHARLES LAIRD, *The Miracle of Language* (New York: A Premier Book, 1953).

5. HALL, *op. cit.*, p. 32.

6. CHARLES C. FRIES, *Linguistics and Reading* (New York: Holt, Rinehart and Winston, 1963), p. 194.

7. BLOOMFIELD AND BARNHART, *op. cit.*, p. 42.

8. *Ibid.*, pp. 57 ff.

9. EMMET A. BETTS, *Foundations of Reading Instruction, With Emphasis on Differentiated Guidance* (New York: American Book Company, 1954).

10. ARTHUR I. GATES, *The Improvement of Reading, A Program of Diagnostic and Remedial Methods* (New York: The Macmillan Company, 1947).

11. WILLIAM S. GRAY, "Better Readers for Our Times," *International Reading Association Conference Proceedings,* Vol. I, (1956). WILLIAM S. GRAY, ed., *Reading in Relation to Experience and Language* (Chicago: The University of Chicago Press, 1944).

12. DAVID H. RUSSELL, *Children Learn to Read,* 2nd ed. (Boston: Ginn and Company, 1961).

13. PAUL A. WITTY, *Reading in Modern Education* (Boston: D. C. Heath, 1949). Also PAUL A. WITTY AND MARGARET RATZ, *A Developmental Reading Program* (Chicago: Science Research Associates, 1956).

14. EDWARD WILLIAM DOLCH, *Teaching Primary Reading,* 3rd ed. (Champaign, Ill.: The Garrard Press, 1960), p. 245.

PART TWO AN OUTLINE
OF THE TEACHING COURSE
IN STRUCTURAL READING

CHAPTER FOUR

The Pre-Reading Program:
From Initial Sounds to Letters

Reading readiness is a prerequisite to the actual teaching of reading. Learning to read requires both maturation and certain well-defined abilities which do not spring forth of themselves on a child's sixth birthday, but must be developed by proper instruction, which, without strain and without drill, will lead naturally to the first steps in reading.

Educators who devise reading readiness programs usually consider the following abilities to be essential for the development of reading readiness: adequate language development, a capacity for visual and auditory discrimination, and interest in learning to read.[1] In many families, parents promote reading readiness by reading and telling stories to their children, encouraging them to participate in family discussions, or stimulating their desire for new experiences by taking them on trips. These children learn to listen, to observe, and to express themselves before they come to school.

Every competent kindergarten teacher makes the most of story periods and reads often to her pupils. She knows how to encourage class discussion and to help children learn to express themselves; this is her opportunity to correct children's pronunciation and to help them speak in clear and precise sentences. In addition, the kindergarten teacher should provide, with all the means at her disposal, whatever experiences will make the life of a child just beginning school interesting and worthwhile. In this way she will give all the different children in her class something of a common background.

Like the well-conducted kindergarten class, the pre-reading program of Structural Reading centers on an oral language-arts program. Each child is encouraged to talk, to express himself in simple but complete sentences; his background is enlarged so that his command of language may be strengthened. Many games (described in Chapter 11) are suggested to the teacher—games designed to enrich children's speaking and comprehending vocabulary.

Further, we strongly believe that a reading readiness program should not end where it usually does. In our pre-reading program the usual readiness activities are included, but we have added activities of much greater scope. The systematic study of sounds heard when words are pronounced, as well as the correspondence between those sounds and the letters that stand for them, can and should be taught as an indispensable part of reading readiness.

Instruction in Structural Reading starts with the identification of the sounds heard in the spoken word, and introduces the letters only afterwards. Children are never asked to stare at printed letters and memorize their names; rather, we begin with meaningful words, helping the child to isolate their initial sounds. Only as a secondary step is a child shown how a sound is recorded by a letter. This procedure finds firm support among linguists. Robert A. Hall writes, "We must make clear from the outset that the reality of language is *sound,* the noises we all make with our faces to communicate with each other, and that letters are simply things which stand for sounds, with much less basic importance than the sounds themselves." [2]

The first games utilized in our method are intended to make children conscious of sounds, that is, to teach them to listen to the sounds made in pronouncing words. As real or pictured objects are named, children's attention is directed to the initial sound heard when each name is spoken. No letters are shown at this stage; the only aim of the game is to develop auditory discrimination. Some of these games are described below.

1 / Listening for Initial Sounds. The teacher displays a number of objects on a tray before the class: a mitten, a candle, a feather, soap, and a leaf. She points to and names the objects, emphasizing the initial sound. Then she starts the game: "The name of the thing I want begins with [f]." Since there is only one object that will fit the sound, the child must select the feather.

2 / Identifying Objects with the Same Initial Sound. The teacher puts three pictures on the board: a lion, a kite, and a lemon. The object is to determine which names start with the same sound. Children think it very amusing that a *l*ion and a *l*emon belong together in this game.

3 / Stories Emphasizing Initial Sounds. The teacher tells several stories in which certain nouns are left unspoken except for their initial sounds. For example, the teacher begins: "Some men went out fishing. They took along a *n* _____." There are of course a lot of things they could have taken with them, fishing rods, or coffee, or blankets, but the [n] suggests a *n*et, which is what the teacher had in mind.

4 / Riddle Game with Initial Sounds. Riddles, too, can be used to develop an ability to discriminate beginning sounds. The teacher poses riddles in which the beginning sound is given as one of the clues: "You sleep in it at night, and it begins with [b]." Or she dismisses the children by using riddles: "The girl with the plaid dress whose name starts with the sound of [b] should now get her coat," or "the boy whose name starts with [f] should now get in line." We have found that children love riddles, and think it amusing that the first sound heard when a word is pronounced may be used as a clue to solve the riddle. They like to invent riddles to ask other children: "It spins. It is a toy and it starts with [t]. What is it?"

While playing these riddle games with the class, the teacher has an excellent opportunity to observe whether or not every child can detect initial sounds. Some children are exceptionally slow in auditory discrimination; they must be taught separately and allowed to proceed slowly.

To help these children, their teacher should start with two initial sounds that differ greatly and choose words she knows are in their vocabularies, such as *f*ire, *f*ox, *f*armer and *m*eat, *m*arbles, *m*ailman. She should pronounce each initial sound as distinctly as possible. If the teacher is patient and does not rush her pupils, even a slow child catches on to this game. When playing these games, teachers should notice whether any child needs special help for correcting speech defects. The earlier a child is sent to a speech specialist, the better is the prognosis, and the easier it is to correct a faulty speech habit.

Teachers are likely to encounter difficulties when parents or older brothers or sisters have taught pupils the alphabet names of letters—for example, that the name *Kathy* starts with the letter "kay" instead of the sound [k]. A child cannot sound out the words *key* or *kite* or *kitten* if he says "kay," rather than [k]. What the teacher must do is disregard the alphabet names for the time being and persist in saying the beginning sounds distinctly and clearly.

As soon as children are able to *hear* initial sounds, they are ready to take the second and more ambitious step of learning how the initial sounds of familiar and meaningful words are recorded by letters. At this point it is not necessary for children to learn either the alphabet as such or the letters in their alphabetical sequence. We determined the order of presentation of the letters followed in the Readiness Book partly by ease of auditory discrimination and partly by the need to keep letters that look somewhat similar far apart (e.g., *b* and *d*).

The purpose of this readiness program is twofold: first, to teach children to recognize and write the letter symbol for each speech sound; second, to broaden their vocabulary range by participating in class discussion of pictures on each page of the Readiness Book.

Some pictures in particular will give teachers the opportunity to acquaint their pupils with unfamiliar objects; this is a very important preparation for subsequent reading. Unless a child knows what is meant by a word, what object it names, he cannot learn to read it comprehendingly; a readiness program should make sure that the words he will be reading will be familiar to him. Edward William Dolch has emphasized how necessary this is: "A word is a symbol for an idea. The idea must be in the mind of the person looking at the word. If the person does not have the idea, the word means nothing." [3]

On the first page of the Readiness Book a picture of a fair appears. Here is an opportunity for much lively discussion. A teacher might ask her class to look for people, objects, or animals whose names start with [m], as *m*onkey, *m*an, *m*ilk bottle, and so on. She would point out that there are balloons, lambs, and flags to be seen and would ask whether the names of these things start with [m], too. After she is reasonably sure that every child can hear which words start with [m] and is able to detect objects that begin with this sound, she can go on to page 2 of the Readiness Book. (See Fig. 4.1.) Here, at the top of the page, there is the key picture for [m], a *m*ask, such as children wear at Halloween. The lines that form the letter which says [m] are part of the *m*ask, thus creating a sensible relationship between the initial sound of *m*ask and the letter *m*. When a child wants to write the letter that says [m], the key picture of the mask will help him recall the form of the letter. A teacher could now write some *m*'s in dotted form on the board and the class can take turns tracing them.

Children will now be ready to name the other pictures on this page: *m*at, *m*atch, *m*ap, *m*ouse, *m*an, etc. They hear that all these words start with the sound [m], the same beginning sound as that of *m*ask. They should then be told to say the name of each picture to themselves, to listen to the beginning sound [m], and to trace the letter *m* that represents the sound. At the bottom of the diagram is an empty line; children should print the letter *m* several times, saying the sound [m] to themselves while they are writing it.* This is important: from the very first children must realize that writing records the sounds they hear in familiar spoken words.

The following excerpts from our records illustrate how this procedure commands children's interest as well as their intelligence. Where letters are italicized, e.g., *c,* they refer to written letters which in this method, throughout grade one, are called by their sound-names, not by their alphabet names.

Peter (5;2) looked at the *f*-page, eager to think of another word. "Flying fish would be good."

When he came to the *s*-page he exclaimed: "Why didn't you think of saddle or saddle shoes for the [s]?"

---

* Writing letters on a given line accustoms children to proceed in the correct left-to-right direction, essential for reading. In addition, writing letters gives the teacher a written record of individual progress and problems.

Fig. 4.1

When Peter learned to write *p* he suddenly looked up and shouted gleefully: "And [p] is for me too!"

In the Readiness Book a test that requires children to say the name of each pictured object and to decide which letter corresponds to each initial sound follows the teaching of every three sounds. Children enjoy these test pages and are proud of how well they perform.

Linda (5;4) came to a test page on September 16th, after eight lessons. "The horse goes to the barn with the *h*; the snake goes to the *s*; the cow goes to the *c*. This is a good page!"

In this readiness program children learn to read initial sounds and to write the letters from *a* to *z*. Their speaking vocabulary is broadened and their ability to express themselves is developed.

Children should be shown that every vowel has a quality that no consonant has. A vowel can be sung, since the tone can be prolonged indefinitely. A consonant, in contrast, is a sound that is blown or mumbled or hissed, as [b] or [m] or [s]. The word *consonant* refers to a letter that gets a clear sound only with or from an accompanying vowel. If Tim is out in the yard, and his mother wants him, she calls "Tiiiiim!" The accent is on the vowel. It is not necessary to go into any greater detail at this point; all that should be done is to give children, upon their first encounter with letters, the idea that vowels have sound qualities that differ from those of consonants. This is most easily done by printing vowels and consonants in different colors. Throughout the Structural Reading Series consonants are printed in blue and vowels in red.

There are a great many games that can be played as soon as letters have been introduced, which are described in detail in Chapter 11. The following record shows how a child's personal experiences can enliven a learning situation.

Derek (5;0), in playing Sound Lotto (see Chapter 11), took out the *m*-card and the *p*-card, calling them *M*ommy-card and *P*appy-card. The teacher had shuffled the corresponding pictures and given them to him. When he found meat, mitten, money, he put them with a smile on the *m*-card, saying: "Mommy likes all these things." Pears, on the other hand, peaches, pineapple, went to the *p*-card. When he then found "plums," he was outraged. "My pappy does not like desserts, I can't give him the plums; he's had enough fruit." So we settled on a pen and a pipe.

The following records of children playing the Snatching Game (see Chapter 11) show that children taught by the Structural Reading method *understand* that each letter has a definite role as the beginning of a familiar word.

Peter (5;3) turned up a card with *c* on it. "It goes with coat," he exclaimed. "I know that one very well." He turned up a picture of a rope and snatched a trick with *r*. "I didn't guess," he said, "I saw the *r*." He turned up a picture of a curtain. "I need a *c* for that curtain."

Michael (5;6) snatched *i* and Indian. I said, "You'll always remember *i* as the beginning of Indian." Michael added, "And as the beginning of ink."

I turned up *p* and took the trick with the picture of a parrot. Michael said, "Or you could have taken the pig."

Linda (5;4) turned up the card with a book on it and took the trick with the *b* in front of her. "Thank you, Mrs. Book, I'm having fun." She took another trick with *l*, explaining "because lamp goes with *l*. You see it starts with [l]." She beamed, "*A* goes with apples because apple begins with [a]."

Linda pointed to the next card. "Is this a house?" "It's supposed to be a store," I explained. "Hah," said Linda, "then I take it with a *s*."

"Gould starts with [g] so *g should* be for you," Linda assured me as I happened to turn up the *g*.

Later I turned up the picture of a garage. Linda said, "There is no *g* on the table, so you don't get a trick."

"I took the *r* with the rooster," Linda exclaimed delightedly. "And now I can take the igloo with the *i*. You are so behind. Whoo, I am lucky."

"*P* and pail, here I go." She took the trick. "Everything goes right for me. Picked up tree: "No *t*'s around here." Turned up *o*: "No ostrich, no octopus. I can't get a trick this time."

The children are eager to think of familiar objects whose names start with a given sound. At the Castle School * each child made his own Sound Book. The pages had one or two lines drawn on them, leaving the rest blank. The teacher wrote a few samples of a particular letter in dotted lines; the child traced these and then wrote the letter himself on the rest of the line. The empty space was used to draw or paste pictures of objects whose names had the initial sound of the written letter.

Mary (5;1) wrote a line of *m*'s and drew a self-portrait (a girl named *M*ary), and then a picture of *M*ommy, and then she had to ask for help. Her daddy belonged to the family picture, and Mary was distressed that neither "*d*addy" nor "*f*ather" started with the required *m*. Finally, she drew a picture of a man and said triumphantly: "Write *M*y Daddy here, then it goes with the *m*."

---

* The Castle School was an experimental school, operated in New York City from 1944-1951 under the guidance of Dr. Catherine Stern, Margaret B. Stern, and Toni S. Gould.

Fig. 4.2 is an example of this kind of work done by Elizabeth, a pupil of Miss Leonore Gordon, P.S. 119, New York City. Elizabeth wrote a line of *r*'s and drew pictures of a *r*abbit, two *r*ed flowers, and two *r*ings, thus showing that she could easily think of objects whose names started with the initial sound [r].

In teaching Structural Reading we introduce the forms of letters simply by letting the five-year-olds *write*. Nothing fixes the form of a letter in the mind better than the kinesthetic experience of writing it repeatedly. This teaching procedure has been vigorously supported by Samuel T. Orton, who advised tracing letters to correct reversals; tracing will establish "the kinesthetic pattern for each letter." [4] The dynamics of writing the letters *b* and *d* serve to show their difference. In contrast, merely looking at the printed forms of *b* and *d* all too often leads to confusion. From an early age, children become accustomed to picture books in which a chicken looks to the left on one page and, on the following page, the chicken looks to the right. The

Fig. 4.2

child recognizes the familiar figures and does not observe their different orientation in space. Why, when a *b* looks to the left (*d*) does it cease to say *b?* This first encounter with the established convention that fixes one orientation for each letter makes no sense to children. Some are proud of being able to recognize the *b* even when it is turned upside down, when it is no longer *b* but *q*. Teachers must expect some children to reverse *b* and *d*, or *p* and *q*, since the forms of the symbols are so similar.

Linda (5;4). "Is it the *d* or the *b?* Which way does the *g* go?" Pointing to the *o* with a sigh of relief, "That can go any way. Some can only go a certain way."

Sometimes in our teaching we give the *b* and *d* special characteristics which can be dispensed with as soon as the children are sure of which way each letter goes. We affix a stroke to the top of the *d*

$$d$$

to represent the head of a *d*uck, our key picture, and we fill in the bottom part of the *b*

$$b$$

to suggest a loaded shopping *b*ag. These devices have proved of tremendous help.

When children hear the sound with which a word starts, when they know which letter stands for that initial sound, when they know how to write each letter, our pre-reading program is accomplished. We strongly urge presenting such a complete pre-reading program in kindergarten, not only to satisfy the active curiosity of most five-year-olds about sounds and letters, but also to pave the way for an interesting and stimulating reading program in Grades One and Two. In our experience we have found that most five-year-olds are able and eager to complete our pre-reading program.

At the Castle School, four- and five-year-olds both enjoyed games with sounds, and in the course of playing such games many learned to read. Parents, teachers, and educators were pleased to see the enthusiasm with which these children read and wrote. More and more frequently in the past few years, experiences similar to ours have been reported—for example, the study conducted by Dolores Durkin.[5]

R. J. Havighurst has invented the illuminating concept of "teachable moments" to describe a period of greatest learning facility.[6] He believes that there is an optimum time to learn a given task, a time when teaching efforts have a maximum potential effect. The same efforts would be wasted if tried before or after a child has reached the required level of maturation.

Teachable moments, however, do not depend only on the time when a certain subject matter has the best chance of being learned. Jerome S. Bruner [7] has made this point in the teaching of science: "Readiness, I would argue, is a function not so much of maturation—which is not to say that maturation is not important—but rather of our intentions and our skill at translation of ideas into the language and concepts of the age we are teaching." This is equally true in the teaching of reading. Learning to read depends not only on maturation but on the *method* by which reading is taught.

If learning to read means learning to memorize the ABC's or the shape of words, then reading instruction can scarcely start late enough. Our pre-reading program, however, captures the interest of the young child, and therefore advances the teachable moment which, with conventional methods of teaching, so often seems out of place and out of reach.

The kindergarten teacher has an entire school year in which to teach each class to listen carefully for sounds and to learn to identify and write the corresponding letters. Our experience indicates that not only bright but also average and even slow children can be taught at this age. They do need not a *later* time but, rather, *more* time to learn than the gifted child. Our experiences have shown that, at the age of five, children with IQ's of 100 or slightly less can learn the correspondence between sounds and letters if given enough time. To wait for the moment when they could learn faster is risky, because often it never seems to come.

Twenty years of teaching experience have shown us that our pre-reading program is of decisive help in preparing all pupils to learn to read. The transition from hearing initial sounds to grasping main word-parts and endings of monosyllabic words, which comes next in the Structural Reading course, is not difficult at all. In fact, reading often comes naturally to our students —something that, one day, one knows without being aware of having made much effort.

Derek, a five-year-old who had learned to read with our method, one day had an urgent question. He said that his sister had suddenly walked at one, and now at two, she was starting to talk. "When," asked Derek, "will the reading come? I forgot how old I was when I could do it."

Reading is, of course, a different process from learning to walk or to talk. Learning to read does not depend on maturation alone, but on adequate preparation and sound teaching. In the Structural Reading course the steps are so carefully planned that a great many children who follow this program discover one day, like Derek, that they are "old enough" to read.

BIBLIOGRAPHICAL NOTES

1. EMMETT A. BETTS, *Foundations of Reading Instruction* (New York: American Book Company, 1946). EDWARD W. DOLCH, *The Psychology and Teaching of Reading* (Champaign, Ill.: The Garrard Press, 1951). ARTHUR I. GATES, *The Improvement of Reading, A Program of Diagnostic and Remedial Methods* (New York: The Macmillan Company, 1947). LUCILLE M. HARRISON, *Reading Readiness* (Boston: Houghton Mifflin Company, 1939). PAUL MCKEE, *The Teaching of Reading in the Elementary Schools* (Boston: Houghton Mifflin Company, 1948). DAVID H. RUSSELL, *Children Learn to Read,* 2nd ed. (Boston: Ginn and Company, 1961).

2. ROBERT A. HALL, JR., *Linguistics and Your Language* (New York: Doubleday & Company, 1960), p. 199.

3. DOLCH, *op. cit.,* p. 176.

4. SAMUEL T. ORTON, *Reading, Writing and Speech Problems in Children* (New York: W. W. Norton and Company, 1937), p. 159.

5. DOLORES DURKIN, "Reading Instruction and the Five-Year-Old Child," *International Reading Association Conference Proceedings,* Vol. VII (1962) , p. 24.

6. ROBERT J. HAVIGHURST, *Human Development and Education* (New York: Longmans, Green and Company, 1953).

7. JEROME S. BRUNER, "On Learning Mathematics," *The Mathematics Teacher,* Vol. LIII, No. 8 (December 1960), p. 617.

CHAPTER FIVE

From the Spoken to the Printed Word

Children's intellects are stimulated and their self-confidence developed when they learn to figure out accurately and with full comprehension what each word on a page says. Their feeling of success so spurs them on that they can hardly wait to tackle page after page.

First, children should discover how to read printed words whose structure corresponds exactly to the structure of the spoken words. We start with the study of monosyllabic words, like *cat, pig, top, mud,* and *hen,* in which each sound heard is represented by one letter with which it corresponds. Because the vowels are the most important characteristic of each of these words, we group words accordingly and teach one such set after the other (ă-group, ĭ-group, ŏ-group, ŭ-group, ĕ-group). We use colored type to emphasize the structure of each word.

Since the children gain insight into the structure of these words, they can write them as well as read them. In this method writing never means simply copying a printed word in script. Writing a word includes the knowledge of how it is constructed, that is, how it is spelled. Because reading, writing, and spelling have an integral structural relationship, they are taught simultaneously.

Our experience has shown that reading not only naturally leads to writing but that the thoughtful building of a word in writing effects, in turn, more efficient reading. This has been substantiated by other investigators in the field, notably Romana B. Spalding.[1]

Before a teacher starts with actual reading instruction, she must find out whether her pupils know how sounds are put down on paper by letters and, conversely, what each letter says. A brief review of sounds and letters should suffice for children who have taken part in our readiness program.

It is imperative that teachers not only understand the vital importance of the beginning program themselves, but also that they help parents and children to understand it. The initial stage of this method may not be as impressive as enabling a child to pretend he can read pre-primers, but in contrast to the sight method, it gives a foundation on which future achievement solidly rests. The foundation of a house may be invisible but it supports even the most imposing structure. In Structural Reading the foundation is solid and leaves no holes which may trip up a child later; it is the groundwork not only for reading but also for writing and spelling.

If there are schools and educators who hesitate to accept the idea of starting with sounds instead of books, let them once more subject to close and honest scrutiny the children, of whom there are far too many, who have failed to learn to read by the sight method. Under optimum home and school conditions, when parents and teachers voice only encouragement and never adverse criticism, a great many children fail and know it because they will compare themselves to those of their peers who have learned how to read. This is damaging to the child's sense of his own adequacy. The fear of failure and the feeling of defeat and despair may mark a child for life. But every child who starts with sounds instead of books gains an immediate feeling of success, which insures his future progress.

If possible, children should never be taught to read simply by repeating what their teacher says. This principle has important implications for the use of signs, experience charts, and books.

Experience charts are composed by teachers from sentences contributed by her class. She writes them down and reads them back. The children take turns "reading" the chart, but most of them are simply reciting from memory. A visitor listening to this recitation might think that some of the children know how to read sentences. Only a very few can in fact do so; the others parrot what they have heard. Experience charts are introduced to enlarge a child's speaking vocabulary by retelling an experience. In addition they are used to fix unfamiliar words, such as *bakery* or *engine*, in memory by connecting them with meaningful experiences. The latter use we deplore. Experience charts that record words children cannot read deprive them of the real value of the recorded experience.

However, experience charts can and should be made vivid and useful by the use of pictures rather than words. A picture of a bakery, farm, or fire station that the class has just visited can be used for lively discussion which will enlarge the children's speaking vocabulary. Written experience charts are not eliminated in the Structural Reading course, but are postponed. Only when a child's reading vocabulary has grown large enough for him to read simple sentences can experience charts be valuable. Then a child not only can contribute to recording his experiences, but will also read his chart with facility and enjoyment.

For similar reasons, children must not be given books at the beginning of first grade. If we start the instruction by teaching the child even as few as thirty sight words, we frustrate his need for discovery; his teacher must identify each word. Postponing the use of books must not mean, however, depriving children of stories. Teachers should frequently read to their classes exciting books suitable to the children's ages and interests, and discuss with them characters and plots.

As we describe the step-by-step teaching procedures of Structural Reading at the first-grade level, one cardinal rule must be kept in mind. All teaching starts with *spoken* words; not, as conventional methods dictate, with printed words.* A few examples of how this is done will be given here.

As the first step, a teacher displays on the board pictures of a man, a cat, and a hat (see Fig. 5.1) and starts a discussion about them, inviting children's comments. She must make sure that each child understands that while a particular picture could be that of a daddy or a postman, in this game it will be called a

---

* The Teacher's Edition of Book B describes in great detail how this is done.

Fig. 5.1

man. We have never had any difficulty with getting children to accept a specific name for a given picture. This preliminary step is of great importance.

Now children are ready to progress to a new game. The teacher asks: "Which picture do I mean if I say [ha t]? The pupil must put the spoken pieces together in his mind to form the familiar word before he can find the right picture.

Since all children have probably heard their mothers call after them, "Take your ha t!," this break seems natural to the child. A speaker likes to dwell on the [ha] before he adds the [t], not only because the vowel gives the word *hat* its special structural characteristic, but because the voice can linger on the [ha]—he can sing a vowel—whereas the final consonant [t] cuts the voice short. When he says [hat] he does not pronounce the sound [h] separately, but ties it to the following vowel; [ha] is heard as the main part of the word *hat.*

The structure of the word *hat* is not revealed by adding up, in piecemeal fashion, the single elements, [h] plus [a] plus [t]; the word divides structurally into a main part [ha] and an ending [t]. The salient point in our method is this emphasis on giving the child insight into the way spoken words break naturally.

It is important that a teacher give each child a turn to lead each game. When a child is able to ask the class, "What do I mean if I say [ca t]," he demonstrates his ability to break a simple monosyllabic word into its component parts. He is, then, prepared to dictate the word [ca t] to himself later, when he will be asked to write it down.

Each day different pictures are displayed. The following list of words suggests appropriate words:

man	rat	hat	cap	bag	pan
cat	bat	map	jam	gas	mat
fan	can	ham	nap	cab	pad

Throughout the Structural Reading course pictures are used to induce children to name the objects that they see and thus pronounce the words before they see them in print. On page 2 of Book B (see Fig. 5.2) there is a series of pictures which the teacher discusses with her class to familiarize the children with the designated name for each picture. Children looking at the picture of a man will say to themselves [man]. Beneath the picture, they will find the written word, broken into two parts:

Fig. 5.2

ma n. The teacher should point out that the printed *ma* beneath the picture says [ma]. Instead of being forced to cope with the irksome blending of [m] and [a], the children are handed, as it were, ready-made blends. Just as on the pre-reading level the children understood [m] or [c] in their function as initial sounds of words, now they will readily grasp [ma] or [ca] in their function as the beginning and main parts of the word *man* or *cat.* As they progress they will discover with interest how the familiar words [hat], [cat], [rat] and [pan] are broken down similarly and recorded as *ha t, ca t, ra t, pa n.*

Quite a few children are delighted when, for the first time, they are able to read these words:

Peter (5;3)	*Read*		*Commented*
	ma n	man	You know it's a boy that's grown-up, like a daddy.
	ca t	cat	A cat! It's an animal.
	ha t	hat	Something that you wear. Ha ha. I am learning to read. Now it's really a reading lesson.

The next step is building words with dominoes, with the aid of the worktext. There is a domino for each of the main parts *ma, ha, ca, ra, pa* and for each ending. Children combine the dominoes to form the words *man, hat,* and so on.

Next, the books are closed, the dominoes mixed up and spread at random on each child's desk. The teacher carefully pronounces one word after the other, separating main part and ending [ma n], and asks the children to build each word she has pronounced with the dominoes. (See Fig. 5.3.) The teacher then prints each word on the board so that the children can check the correctness of what they have built. Finally, the children take turns reading the words and should be encouraged to show their comprehension by commenting on them.

Building the word *man* with dominoes with self-dictation is excellent preparation for learning how to write *man.* It is a way of teaching the *thinking* part of writing while eliminating the strain of forming the needed letters, which detracts from the thinking process. When a child reaches this point, he will have a twofold preparation for writing the first words: (1) he will have learned in the readiness program the mechanics of

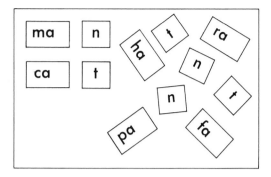

Fig. 5.3

writing the letters, and (2) he will have learned how to build up each word from the domino games.

Writing is started on the same page as reading. Pictures, such as those at the bottom of Fig. 5.2 are used to elicit spoken words. As each child names a picture and *listens to himself,* he writes down what he has said, which is a familiar word he has built before with dominoes.

From the start each child must learn to write from his own dictation. If he wants to write *hat,* he should think first of its beginning [ha] and, as he says it to himself, immediately write *ha.* After *ha* is written he will stop to say the word again, but now emphasizing the last sound [ha*t*], to finish the word with the letter *t.* He is able to write the end-sound *t* without hesitation, since the end-consonant of every word is clearly pronounced. He finds the task easy, since it calls for correspondence between the heard sound and the written letter, a correspondence he has already learned.

One interesting phenomenon is to be observed. The child has met and absorbed *ca* as a whole and as the beginning of *ca t,* when he saw it printed below the picture and on one domino. But when he starts to write *ca,* he becomes aware that it requires *two letters, c* and *a.* Experience has shown that this fact is much easier to grasp than its opposite, that is, to learn to blend *c* and *a* to form [ca].

It is fascinating, at this point in the course, to see a child *think* while he is writing down his first words. He is not struggling to remember a fixed but meaningless sequence of letters.

He has learned how the spoken word he is now writing is built up, and he is confident that by listening to himself he can translate the spoken word into the written word. He will not make spelling mistakes because in this method spelling is the result of *knowing* how a word is built up.

This is in striking contrast to the usual procedure, according to which children are asked to copy a word or to spell a word by remembering a succession of letters.

The teacher dictated, "A cat sat." Peter (5;4) wrote this sentence down, and commented, "I know how to write *sat* very easily. See I sound out the words, and then I know how to spell them."

Children who are taught spelling by drill make senseless errors, as the following episode illustrates.

While playing a game called Writing Stories (see Chapter 11) the five-year-olds at the Castle School wrote the word *dog*. Enid, an older sister who had come to visit that day, asked to be allowed to participate in this activity. She wrote *boy* and then showed the paper to the teacher: "Does this say *dog* or *boy*? I always mix them up."

No child who has been taught to analyze the word *dog* could possibly mistake it for *boy*. To illustrate this point, here is a comment made by one of our pupils.

Peter (5;5) wrote *dog*. "I know that this spells dog because I know the [do] is the beginning and it has a [g] at the end."

Of course, children taught by any method will occasionally make mistakes, but the errors children make when taught by a method based on memorizing are *blind* errors. Children who have learned by insight will make errors when their attention momentarily lapses, but their teachers need only direct them to read what they have written, and they will immediately recognize and correct their mistakes.

A further advantage of this method is that the teacher is provided with a written record of each child's performance. Errors are recorded and can be discussed with each child. The teacher must *not* correct a mistake by saying the right word, but must insist that the child find and correct the error himself.

Instead of asking the teacher for help when they need it, children can, by themselves, look up the word they want in the *Picture Dictionary* (see Chapter 11). The function of this dictionary is to make children independent in reading and writing.

To give children further practice at this stage we have devised additional domino games, which are described in Chapter 11. Here are some remarks made by children while they were playing these games. Here, too, we see children's lively interest and full comprehension.

Katherine (4;6) named the pictures that the teacher had placed in a row in front of her. Then the dominoes with *ca, ma, fa,* etc. were placed face downward on her table and the dominoes with the end-sounds were openly displayed.

Katherine took up *ca* and said: "[Ca]! I can use it for [cat] or [can]." She turned up *ma* and said: "[Ma]! I can use it for [mat] or [man]."

Two weeks later, she played the same game with more pictures. She turned up *fa;* "[fa]! I can use it for fan!" She placed it on the proper picture, silently adding the *n.*

She read: "[ba]! I can use it for bat." She placed it on the picture, and completed the word with *t.* "[Ma]! I can use it for man." She found the *n* to complete the word. "[Ca]! I can use it for cat." She looked for and added the *t.*

These and other games, described in Chapter 11, have always succeeded in teaching our pupils to recognize a main word part at a glance.

Until now, all words have been printed in broken parts, showing their main parts and their endings separately. Children are now ready to go to the next step—to be confronted for the first time with the task of reading ă-words as a whole. This excerpt from our records shows how one child handled page 5 in Book B (see Fig. 5.4), the page in the worktext that covers these words.

Katherine (4;6) looked at the first word and said: "fa n, fan!" She looked at the picture and exclaimed joyfully, "And a fan!" She went on, "Ma n, man, and now the picture—a man! It's just the same!" She continued: "Pa n, pan! (pointing to the picture) and a pan!" She came to the next word. "Ca n, can!—and there is the picture of a can!"

Every child is delighted to find that he can say what a printed word indicates and that its picture confirms what he has read. At this stage many a child would rather utilize his ability to figure out the word than rely on the picture.

Peter (5;3) pointed to a poorly drawn picture in the draft of our workbook. "Is it a pot or a pan?" He was asked to find out himself

fan

man

pan

can

van

Fig. 5.4

by reading. He studied the word, saying, "Pa n, pan! It's a pan!" He exclaimed delightedly, "I am really learning. These games make you learn to read."

Soon all children are ready to read words without the help of pictures. A teacher should write the words already studied on the board, using blue chalk for the consonants and red chalk for the vowels; children should then be given turns to read the words. If some hesitate, there is a simple way to help them. The teacher should cover the end-consonant; the child reads *fa*. The end is uncovered and the child reads the word: fa*n*.

For quite a time many children will read a printed word such as *map* in two pieces (*ma p*), but will then immediately repeat it as a whole word with the right intonation, and show by their comments that they understand its meaning. Our case studies indicate that Structural Reading prevents meaningless *word calling;* some records follow which illustrate this point.

	Sounded out	Pronounced word correctly	Gave meaning of word
Katherine (4;6)			
	ca n	can!	Drinking a can of tomato juice.
	ma p	map!	You need it when you are lost on the road.
	ma n	man!	A man that walks.
	ba t	bat!	A bat—what you bat a ball with.
	ha m	ham!	Ham, you eat it!
	ha t	hat!	Hat, what you wear on your head.
	fa n	fan!	A fan—the house is hot, you need a fan.
Jeff (5;1)			
	na p	nap!	Well, you go to sleep!
	ma t	mat!	A mat to step on outside.
	ma n	man!	A man works.
	ba t	bat!	A bat, you use it to swing a baseball.
	ra t	rat!	Well, it steals— its best meat is cheese.
	ca t	cat!	A cat—it says meow.
	ma p	map!	A map! You look at it to find out where another country is.
	ca p	cap!	You put it on your head!

Sounded out	*Pronounced word correctly*	*Gave meaning of word*
Ken (5;7)		
ma n	man!	A real man!
ha m	ham!	A lovely piece of ham to eat.
na p	nap!	If we have a nap we rest.
ha t	hat!	Which my daddy puts on his head.
ma p	map!	Where you see where you want to go.
la p	lap!	Like, we sit on Mommy's lap.
ca n	can!	A can of juice.

If one listens to a child at this stage of reading, one can still hear a last trace of the pause between [ma] and [n]. The next goal is to assist the progress from this stage of putting word-parts together to fluent reading.

To test reading accuracy children are given pages with words in the left-hand column and pictures in the right-hand column. But now, word and opposite picture do *not* match. The child reads each word silently to himself and is told to draw a line from each word to its corresponding picture.

For additional practice, we distribute sheets of paper to a class on which previously studied words are written. The children are to read each word and illustrate it, thus proving their comprehension. Fig. 5.5 is a diagram, done by a pupil of Miss Edith Wilson at P.S. 90 in New York City, that shows how well children can perform this task.

Fig. 5.5

Through practice children learn to recognize at a glance the familiar words which they have studied so carefully. For most children, sight-reading starts by itself without any help; it is a natural endproduct of studying, reading, and writing each word. Since, however, reading words at sight is necessary before children can advance to reading sentences, we have devised games that aid all children to reading at sight. (See Chapter 11.)

It must be noted that there is a distinct difference between the haphazard sight vocabulary established in the usual basal reading series and the sight words in Structural Reading. In the sight method, sight reading forms the starting point of instruction; the beginning reader is confronted with words that he is expected to memorize by rote. In contrast, in the Structural Reading method, sight reading is the culmination of a learning process based on insight and discovery. All words have been carefully analyzed before they are read at sight and can be sounded out if necessary. It is of vital importance that a teacher herself understand how this method differs not only from the sight method but from the usual phonetic methods as well. Superficially, the teaching pages of Book B may not seem to differ from the usual phonic drill book; they do differ radically, however, and if they should ever be used for phonic drill all the advantages that derive from teaching by giving insight into word structure would be lost. Neither phonic drill nor flash-card drill of sight words are needed or can be permitted in this method of teaching.

In describing this course, we have taken the $\breve{a}$-group as the example for describing the basic steps that lead from the analysis of the spoken word to the instant identification of that word in print. In each unit ($\breve{i}$-group, $\breve{o}$-group, $\breve{u}$-group, and $\breve{e}$-group) the child advances by the same steps to fluent reading of the words at sight. After all these short-vowel groups have been studied, children know about 100 words "at sight." However, each of these 100 words can be sounded out, read intelligently, and written down.

After each group of words is introduced, the words in it are used in sentences. How the structure of a sentence is grasped is described in the next chapter. But before a child can begin to read sentences, we must be sure that he can read *each word* of a sentence independently and accurately. The beginning reader must continue reading *one word* at a time with full comprehension before he begins reading sentences. This is in direct contrast to the lamentable practice of teaching children to read sentences while he can as yet only guess what the words say. To begin the teaching of reading by concentrating not on complete sentences but on single words is in complete harmony with the development of each child. To the young child, a word always brings to mind a complex of ideas. The toddler who is just starting to talk uses one-word sentences, as it were, to express his wishes and observations. Similarly, a single word read by a child with understanding suggests to him a complete thought, sometimes even an entire story. The comments made by our articulate pupils show this to be true. No word calling is allowed in Structural Reading; the meaning of each word is comprehended from the very first step. At whatever level we observe a child, whether he can read *cat* and *fan, cot* and *top,* or has advanced to *cane* and *gate,* our basic procedure is the same. A child gains insight into the structure of the words that belong to the new group, and this insight helps him decipher an unfamiliar but structurally related word by himself with full comprehension.

Since we use pictures to introduce words, in the early stages of the course we teach only the names of objects, that is, nouns. But the skill that children develop in sounding out unfamiliar words enables them to read adjectives like *fat* or *sad* or some verb forms like *ran* or *sat.* Children show their comprehension by their comments.

Katherine (5;1) read *fat* for the first time. "Oh fat! Someone is eating too much!"

Michael (5;9) figured out *sad* by himself when the teacher wrote the word on a piece of paper: "Sa d, sad! If you are unhappy!"

We have found the same phenomenon of transfer effective in moving from one group of words to the next. Many children do not need any help in deciphering the words in the *ĭ*-group, since they mastered the principle of how to sound out words when they studied the *ă*-group.

Wendy (5;2) read the words on the page (p. 29 of Book B), saying delightedly, "I read them. I don't look at the pictures any more!"

When Willa (6;6) started studying the ŭ-group (pp. 81–84) she caught on immediately. "I don't want to see the pictures. I just want to read."

When George (4;6) was studying the ŏ-words, he came across the word *not* for the first time. He read *not* and said mischievously, "Somebody should *not* do bad things; that's me!"

If a child taught by the sight method came upon the unfamiliar word *not* in a sentence or story, he would stare at the word and try to remember what the teacher called it. Was it *but, hot, net* or *no?* He might guess from the context what it says, but he might as easily guess wrong. In Structural Reading a child does not guess; he deciphers the words and then puts them into context. George, in the instance cited above, shows how his mind is at work developing a meaningful context. He knows with certainty how to decode the written word he has not read before. His intelligence as well as his imagination are called into play, and his remarks prove that he fully comprehends what he has read.

BIBLIOGRAPHICAL NOTE

1. ROMANA B. SPALDING, WITH WALTER T. SPALDING, *The Writing Road to Reading* (New York: Whiteside Inc., and William Morrow & Company, 1957).

CHAPTER SIX

From Reading Words to Reading Sentences and Stories

When the child has learned to decipher single words, he has mastered the necessary first step toward reading sentences. But that he has taken only the first step, and that the next step will require him to learn a more complex skill, must be borne in mind. A child who reads a sentence word by word, as if each were of the same importance, is reading as if he were arranging single beads in a row, instead of stringing the beads together to form a necklace. It is not enough to be able to read each word separately; the child must learn to grasp the thought that strings the words together into a coherent sentence.

Every sentence consists of a group of words which in their totality express a complete thought. Each word, then, must be understood not only for the meaning it has in itself, but for the role it plays in the sentence. The child must learn to extract the meaning of the sentence as a whole. Thus, reading sentences requires more mental effort than reading words; the child will learn to take one step more toward developing the power that eventually will enable him to read books intelligently.

As long as the child was studying single words, he was free to associate any given word with whatever image came first to mind. That is, he could put the word into any context he liked. Reading the word *hat,* for instance, he could think of his own hat, of Mommy's or Ann's hat, of "The Cat in the Hat." But now, when he reads the simple sentence, "Dad has a hat," he must limit his ideas to one hat out of all the hats in the world: Dad's hat. Learning to read sentences, then, requires that the child learn how to interpret exactly what meaning the author intended.

In teaching this next step, it is important to understand how the course of instruction in Structural Reading differs, as it did in the earlier steps, from both the sight and the phonics approaches. The proponents of the sight approach advocate the use of single sentences as one of the *first* steps in reading. The sentences presented contain a great many words that the child cannot yet decipher by himself. The child does not read the sentence; he repeats what the teacher says. In Structural Reading, however, the sentences are composed only of words the child can read.

The usual phonics teacher—with the exception of Mae Carden —seems to assume that the only requirement for the fluent reading of a sentence is the ability to read separate words. This is not so. Often a child who has been taught in this way correctly reads aloud one word, then the next and the next, but the expression on his face shows clearly that he has no insight into the meaning of the sentence. He has learned to read *words*—not sentences.

A beginner often reads each word in a sentence with *equal emphasis*, although of course he does not speak that way. When he tells his mother: "I want some milk," he pronounces "I" "want" and "some" with almost the same force, and then gives emphasis to the climactic word of the sentence, "milk." The teacher must teach the child to read sentences as he speaks them— with a varied intonation. It is not enough to simply read each word, however fluently; the voice must bring out what the mind finds important. For the adult to whom reading sentences seems a natural outcome of reading words, we shall illustrate the child's predicament by taking him through a somewhat similar experience.

Read the following:

> *read to learn to*
> *want not do I said*
> *Sam.*

Although you can read each word correctly, all together the words do not make sense. You are vaguely aware that the text is concerned with Sam, that somebody called "I" said something, that reading and learning were mentioned. Now read the sentence backwards, from right to left, from the lower line to the one above, starting with the word *Sam*. You may find that you read more slowly than usual, although now you can grasp the meaning.

The words of the sentence were presented in the wrong sequence to force you to read each word separately and to show you how this makes it impossible to interpret the text. All too often, the child attacking his first sentence has a similar experience. At this stage the child will read haltingly, dwelling on one word at a time, and thus may not be able to make sense of the whole sentence. The skill of reading sentences is a new departure for the child, and it must be taught gradually and systematically. In Structural Reading sentences are introduced immediately after the short-*a* words are learned. By restricting ourselves to sentences containing only short-*a* words, the child, knowing the words, can concentrate on getting the meaning of the sentence.

The children themselves sense the tremendous step from reading single words to grasping the thought presented by even the simplest sentence. This is how one child felt about learning to read new words and then about his first sentences.

Jeff (5;2)	*Read*	*Commented*
	la p lap	It's your lap.
	Sa m Sam	It's a name.
	Sam ha s a ca t, Sam has a cat!	I guess I really can read real words!
	Sam has a ma t, Sam has a mat!	
	Sam has a ba t. A bat; Sam has a new bat!	
	Sam has a na p. Sam has a nap.	Boy, this is real reading!

It is true that the sentences to which we are limited by the Structural Reading method are extremely simple, since the vocabulary does not allow for a colorful command of language. A sentence like "a man sat" or "a cat ran" has neither literary value nor an exciting tale to tell the child. However, it would be a grave mistake to postpone the teaching of sentences until more words are learned, since learning to read sentences is so vital a part of the reading process and absolutely integral to it. In the Structural Reading method this deficiency is counteracted by incorporating the simple sentences in an amusing context. In the workbooks the meager sentences are used as significant parts of interesting tasks which the children enjoy.

In Structural Reading each new step begins with the spoken word. Accordingly, the preparation for reading sentences must also begin on the spoken level. The teacher should draw attention to a child who *has* a red dress and to another who *has* a new box of crayons. She writes the new word *has* on the board, the children read it by sounding it out (ha s); they then understand its meaning. By itself, *has* does not stand for any tangible object. When the teacher writes the sentence "Ann has a cat," the word *has* links the two nouns, and the whole sentence tells what Ann "has" or owns. When the teacher writes similar sentences on the board, they are easily read and fully understood.

Page 17 of Book B (see Fig. 6.1) presents such sentences. The text offers two endings to a sentence which begins with the words, "Dad has." Although a child could recite quickly and without prompting a lot of things that Dad "has," he must decide whether "a nap" or "a hat" makes sense in the given situation. The child chooses the correct ending by looking at the picture, which shows that he does *not* have a nap but that he is wearing a hat. In completing each of the sentences, the child is given a choice between two possible objects a person may have. He must read each sentence wth each alternative ending and then, looking at the picture, decide which ending is right.

The records of children tackling this page show their comprehension. Emily deliberated out loud which choice was correct.

Emily (5;8)	*Read*	*Commented*
	Dad has a nap.	He is *not* taking a nap. He is walking. But he has a hat.
	Ann has a bag.	That's it. She has a bag. A bag is something you carry things in. You can either call it a purse or a bag. Well, a pad is something that you draw on, and she doesn't have that.

Sam has a pan.   I don't think he'd have a pan. That would be funny if he did. A baseball player using a pan for cooking. He has a bat.

Nan has a tag.   Nan has a tag? She doesn't have a tag, does she? She has a cat. She is taking it for a walk or something.

Dad has ----- a nap
                a hat

Ann has   a bag
           a pad

Sam has   a pan
           a bat

Nan has   a tag
           a cat

Fig. 6.1

Page 20 of Book B shows five portraits: Dad, three boys, and one girl. There is room under each picture to write the name of each person; but "who is who?" When the child reads that Sam has a pack, that Dan has a cap, and Jack has a sack, he can identify each individual from the description in the sentence. The teacher can check the child's comprehension of the sentence by seeing if the correct name is written underneath each picture. (See Plate 2.)

Here is how Emily handled this page.

Emily (5;9)	*Read*	*Commented*
	Sam has a pack.	A pack is something you carry things in. This is Sam because he has the pack.
	Dan has a cap.	This is Dan because he has a cap, and no one else has a cap.
	Jack has a sack.	This is Jack, because he has a sack—he might have potatoes in it.
	Ann has a fan.	I know why that's Ann because she is the only one who has a fan.
	Dad has ham.	Here is Dad, because he is the only one who has the ham.

The organization of the Structural Reading worktexts provides the teacher with another advantage. The reading of the text is followed by a written sequel which inevitably discloses whether the meaning of the text was fully grasped. Thus the teacher has a written record of each pupil's performance. Mistakes can be discussed with the individual child. In this way the teacher will be able to determine if the errors were caused by carelessness or by some uncertainty which must be remedied by additional help.

Plate 2 also serves to illustrate the difference between the sight approach and Structural Reading. A child who is learning by sight may read *sack* instead of *pack* without knowing he has made a mistake, since both words will fit the same context. The sight-reading primers do not force the child to realize that careless reading or guessing may lead him into error.

In contrast, the tasks on the pages of the Structural Reading

Series are designed so that *each word must be read accurately* for the child to arrive at a satisfactory solution. If the child reads *sack* for *pack* on the *Who is Who?* page, he would not be able to identify Sam or Jack correctly. Thus the child is made to realize that guessing at words is *not* reading; if he makes a careless mistake, he will correct his error by sounding out the word carefully, thus arriving at the exact word the author has written. Even when words are being read at a glance, the sounding-out technique is used to rectify mistakes or to resolve doubts. The thorough study of a word not only helps to correct errors but also leads to accurate reading the next time the word is encountered: the child *learns* from his errors.

To give additional practice in grasping sentences instantly we have used a question-and-answer game which children greatly enjoy. The teacher asks a question and writes on the board the sentence—to be read by the child—that gives the answer. The teacher asks the class, for instance, "What does Sam have?" She writes the answer on the board: "Sam has a cat." The question gives a frame of reference—the children will expect the written sentence to tell what "Sam has." Consequently, the written sentence will be instantly understood and fluently read.

Here's an example that shows how much the children enjoy this game.

The teacher asked Katherine: "What does Ann have for supper?" Katherine read, "Ann has ham"—and she continued, "and when Ann has ham we like some too." The teacher then asked: "What does Ann play with?" Katherine read, "Ann has a cat," and added "to play with."

This question-and-answer game is also very helpful in teaching children to write sentences without any samples to copy from and without the dictation of the teacher. The children listen to a question, think of an answer, and write it down.

The sentences become more interesting after action words can be introduced. For the first time the child must focus his attention not only on the subject shown in a picture but on the action too. One of the pictures on p. 24 of Book B shows a man, and the pupil must write the word *man* in the blank space below the picture. The sentence ends with the word *ran,* which the children will know how to decipher by transfer (ra n). They will understand that this word refers to the action of the man in the picture. In another sentence the same man is shown, and again the word *man* must be written beneath the picture. But now he is sitting on a chair and the concluding word *sat* tells what he is doing. By asking the children questions about these sentences, the teacher can ascertain their comprehension. Children like to talk about what they have read.

Emily (5;9)	*Read*	*Commented*
	A man ran.	I get it. . . . He ran. Sometimes when you are scared you run away from a person.
	A man sat.	Now the man is sitting. He is not running any more.

As the children study each succeeding workbook page, the teacher provides additional practice by writing on the board sentences that use the vocabulary learned to date. She must challenge the children's intellectual powers by asking them to contribute comments on each sentence. By using their speaking vocabulary, they put the simple sentence into a broad context.

Katherine (5;8)	*Read*	*Commented*
	Sam has a bat.	Hit, hit, hit!
	Ann has a fan.	She needs it in the summer.
	Sam ran	. . . to his home.
	A man ran.	That is funny. He ran over to the Roberts.
	A cat sat.	She sat on a cushion.
	A man sat	on a chair.
	A rat ran	to the barn.

As the children advance, step by step, from the study of the ă-group to the ĭ-, ŏ-, ŭ-, and ĕ-words, the sentences become more varied. With the introduction of the ĭ-words, the sentences can make use of the word *is*. Again, we show how a child proves her comprehension by her comments.

Katherine (5;8)	*Read*	*Commented*
	Ann is mad.	Someone took Ann's toys away.
	Dad is sad	'cause the cows are lost.
	Pat is fat	'cause he ate too much.

It is important to encourage the children to use their imaginations. We have quoted many instances to show how children like to comment on the simple sentences they are reading. Some children are able to go beyond this stage; they connect the separate sentences and invent their own stories. Here is an example from our records:

George (4;6)	*Read*	*Commented*
	Sam has a cat.	
	The cat had ham.	
	Sam hit the cat	. . . because the cat ate all the ham.
	The cat is sad.	The cat is sad because Sam hit him.
	The cat ran to Sam	. . . so to be friends again.
George (4;7)		
	Bob hit the dog.	
	The dog bit Bob	. . . because he hit him.
	The dog hid in a tub	. . . because he did not want Bob to know where he was.

It is important to encourage the invention of stories from simple facts, to stimulate the powers of the child's imagination. On the other hand, the children must be prepared to read information exactly; they must learn that every word is significant and must be understood with precision. The children must discover how each word in a sentence contributes to its meaning and specificity. On page 26 of Book B (see Plate 3), there are pictures of eight cats. When the sentence starts with the words "a cat," any of the cat pictures may stand for these two words. The next line adds one word, "a *fat* cat"; now only three pictures fit, those that show a cat that is fat. "A fat cat sat" applies only to the two fat cats that are not running, but sitting. Finally, the child reads: "A fat cat sat at the rag bag." Now there is only one cat that answers the description. The child has been shown how important a role *each word* plays in this sentence; if he misreads even *one* word (as children often do in schools where guessing is encouraged) the sentence is misinterpreted.

At this stage children like to illustrate sentences. This is not only a worthwhile task but a valuable test of their sentence comprehension. This sort of project has been adapted for the use of large classes by presenting sentence strips printed on butcher paper. The children show by their illustrations that they have learned to read and to understand sentences. The following illustrations are samples chosen from those drawn by children taught with this method in a pilot project in New York City. (See Figs. 6.2 and 6.3.) *

Fig. 6.2

---

* The following teachers participated in this project and submitted the illustrations carried out by their pupils:

Mrs. Edna Blutman, P.S. 175, New York, Fig. 6.2, drawn by Edith.
Miss Maureen Carraher, P.S. 39, New York, Fig. 6.3, drawn by Mary.

At a later stage children write their own sentences and illustrate them. (See Fig. 6.4, Plate 5, Plate 6.) * The teacher writes on index cards the words the children cannot yet spell and explains their structure. At this time many children like to start their own dictionaries filing newly discovered words for later use.

At this stage of the course in Structural Reading, experience charts serve a useful purpose. After the class has undertaken a trip, the teacher can record the experiences on a chart. Her job is

The pig has a bib

Fig. 6.3

Miss M. Purtell, P.S. 175, New York, Fig. 6.4 drawn and written by Marion.

Mrs. Gertrude K. Wiesenfeld, P.S. 90, New York, Plate 5, drawn and written by Charles.

Mrs. Dorothy Whittington (co-author of the Structural Reading Series teacher's guides) Plate 6, drawn and written by Susie, public school in Seattle.

Fig. 6.4

to supply familiar words whenever possible or to introduce any new words by pronouncing them carefully, writing them on the board, and analyzing their structure.

To give further practice in sentence comprehension, we have prepared some booklets as supplementary reading to the Structural Reading Series worktexts. One sentence of a story is printed on each successive page until the whole story is told. The children are instructed to draw a picture illustrating each sentence. The illustrations show whether the children have read each sentence correctly and with full comprehension. In studying the children's illustrations the teacher may learn a great deal about each individual child. There are children who merely transmit the written text to the page by drawing the bare content. Imaginative children may draw a picture that they created in their minds while reading the text, embellishing it. We reproduce here the illustrations of one little girl who made these drawings for one of our first booklets. (See Fig. 6.5 drawn by Doon.)

From concentrating on sentences, the child progresses to read simple stories and to grasp their content as a whole. Here again, instruction should start on the spoken level. The teacher should frequently tell simple stories to the class, interrupting herself and asking the children to figure out what might happen next. This gives the children insight into the structure of a story. It is much easier to remember and to analyze a narrative told by the teacher than to struggle with the mechanics of reading a text and to grasp its content at the same time.

In the Structural Reading Series the first stories are simple narratives in which each sentence develops the plot. Here is one of the stories (from page 51 of Book B) and the comprehension questions that accompany it.

THE BAT

Sam hid the bat.
Bill is mad.
"Give back the bat," said Bill.
"I will," said Sam.
Bill is back at bat.

Who Is It?

Who hid the bat? _____
Who is mad? _____

Sentences presented in Book B prior to these stories have an arbitrary order. On page 20 of Book B (see Plate 2), for instance, it makes no difference if Ann is found before Jack, or Dad before Dan. A story, however, hangs together; each sentence has the function of telling the reader what happens next. The children learn to anticipate what each additional sentence will say. They soon realize that a story has a beginning and an end.

The teacher should use stories such as "The Bat" to demonstrate that in a story the sentences are not interchangeable. "Bill is mad" makes sense only if it follows "Sam hid the bat." And "I will" must come after "Give back the bat." Only the logical

Tom's cap

Tom got a re[d] cap.

Tom met Rex.
Tom and Rex ran.

Tom lost his red cap.

Fig. 6.5

Tom was sad.
The red cap was
lost.

ex ran up the
ill to hunt for
he cap.

ex ran to Tom
e had the red
ap.

Fig. 6.5 (continued)

order of the sentences develops the plot by showing cause and effect.

Children like to experiment with the order of sentences in a story, and learn that when this order is disrupted the sense is changed or destroyed. Such experiences give children insight into the necessity of telling a story by arranging sentences in the correct plot sequence.

As the known vocabularly increases (see Chapter 7) the reading material becomes more complex. Where one sentence had been used to carry the narrative forward, now several sentences, in a paragraph, express one narrative step. Clear thinking is required to understand the ideas contained in the paragraph.

The teacher should check and develop comprehension by asking the children to sum up in their own words the information given. She will quickly discover which children need extra help.

As more facts are told and more details are given, a child may easily lose the narrative thread. The child must be taught from the very first not only to read with understanding but to anticipate what might come next, so that the succeeding part will be easily intelligible.

Slow children, however, will need extra help in making the transition from comprehending simple, single sentences to grasping the meaning of the story as a whole. It is hard for them to keep what they have read in mind and to understand the plot as a whole, and not as a disconnected series of events. The teacher should help by interrupting the child after he has read one paragraph, and ask him to tell in his own words what the story has said so far. After this, she should invite him to figure out what might happen next. This not only deepens his understanding of what he has already read but also sets the stage for the events to come.

The teaching of reading in the classroom must develop two different skills: silent reading and oral reading. At the beginning, the sounding-out process necessitates articulation. In order to avoid the disturbance that would result from every child reading aloud at once, the teacher should teach the children to sound the words out by using their "inner voice," that is, by keeping their sounding-out inaudible. They must learn to listen carefully as they talk to themselves; the teacher will see how soon their lips move quietly and their voices are hushed. As soon as the sounding-out process is replaced by sight-reading, even that "inner voice" must be silenced. The expert reader will grasp meaning directly, as his eyes move along the lines. Slow readers often have difficulty with giving up silent articulation. If each word must be separately pronounced, reading speed cannot be rapid. It is most important that the teacher help all her pupils to develop the ability to dispense with the sounding-out process. Many pages in the worktext can be reused to teach and check this indispensable skill.

To offer but one example: After the word *give* has been introduced in *We Discover Reading* the teacher tells the children to turn back to page 25, where the names Ann, Dan, Sam, and Jan appear with a picture accompanying each name. She then writes on the board the following sentences, one at a time: "Give Ann a bag. Give Dan a cap. Give Sam a fish. Give Jan a cat." The pupils look at each instruction she has written and draw the required object. The teacher must make clear to her class that only silent reading is to be allowed. No murmur should be heard and no lips should move.

While the skill of silent reading is being mastered, the second skill, that of oral reading, should be introduced. Oral reading is reading aloud with intelligent expression, a quite different thing from the sounding-out of words with which the reading process began. The object of that first reading aloud was to assist the child in deciphering words; the object of oral reading is to improve and to demonstrate reading comprehension.

The teacher should begin teaching this skill by reading a text first without and then with correct intonation, and should then ask the class to decide which rendition seems right.

I read Kathy (6;6) a poem in a monotonous voice, without any expression, and then asked her:

I: Is that the way to read a poem?
Kathy: Nobody can understand it.
I: How would you read it?

Kathy read it beautifully, bringing out with her voice the important points.

I: How does one read a poem?
Kathy: Slowly and in different tones, sometimes pausing—some kind of wavy—fast and slow!

Children especially enjoy reading aloud nonsense jingles such as those in Plate 4 (from page 76 of Book B). In reading them, children demonstrate whether they have understood how to bring out the humor of each jingle or whether they still need additional help. It is well known that six-year-olds enjoy absurdities. The following example was taken from our records.

Willa (6;6)	*Read*	*Commented*
	Can a dog live on a rock?	No, it would die from hunger. It would die from thirst. It cannot! It cannot!

As the children progress, the tests more and more resemble stories and poems found in books written for children's pleasure. By the end of the first grade a veritable reading explosion occurs. Children suddenly break loose! To their own delight and that of their parents and teachers, the children discover that they can read books! Easy books or primers of all kinds—which should be made available in the classroom at this time—are devoured steadily with mounting enthusiasm.

Peter (5;9) read the first few pages of *Tip* with me and then passed the book to me commenting: "It's easy to do it at home, because it's easy, but I don't want to spend my time in the lesson doing it."

At this point children try to read whatever comes into their hands, and no longer have to limit themselves to reading our worktexts. It is a great event in the child's life to be able to read on his own. If they cannot read a new word they can ask the teacher for help, but they rarely seem to need any. Miraculously, the mastery of sounding out words plus the understanding of the content of a story make most children able to decipher new words by themselves.

We could add pages of examples to show the amazing skill of our pupils in figuring out words they have never seen before. Because they have a sure command of the learned vocabulary, new words are relatively few and can be readily deciphered by sounding out. Occasionally a phonetic irregularity makes it impossible to arrive at better than an approximation of the word; in such cases the children are usually able to correct themselves, since they know which familiar word, whose approximate pronunciation they have discovered, would fit the context of the story. Our records give ample evidence of the confidence with which children enlarge their reading vocabulary by themselves once a secure foundation is laid.

Thus far, we have focused our attention on the development of the ability to read sentences and stories; one important problem remains which demands discussion. Too often, there is a deplorable gap between a child's genuine interests and the reading ability needed to satisfy them. Children can be starved by meager texts which use controlled vocabularies, or frustrated when they lack the skill to read books whose contents fascinate them. By the time they acquire the ability to read beginning books with ease, they may have outgrown the simplicities of the primers, but are not yet able to read well enough to follow the texts of books that really interest them. The course in Structural Reading closes this gap successfully. The ability to read is developed so rapidly that children are not hindered from reading books written for their age levels.

After a solid foundation in reading instruction has been laid, books that contain words not yet encountered may be offered. Many of the children are so proficient in sounding out words that they can read phonetically irregular words on their own. There were quite a few children who, while still studying worktext C, avidly read books without further help.

The whole class, however, should now branch out to read books with interesting plots since, at this stage of learning, practice in reading books brings about the perfection of the accomplished reader. As soon as the children have thoroughly understood the function of the magic *e* individualized reading instruction should be started. In such a program the children work independently, at their own rate, often in groups, and proceed to various Beginner Books * according to their abilities. In one of our pilot projects seven of the easier Beginner Books were selected as the core of the program.

1. *Green Eggs and Ham* by Dr. Seuss
2. *Ten Apples Up On Top* by Theodore Le Sieg
3. *Go, Dog, Go* by P. D. Eastman
4. *Put Me in the Zoo* by Robert Lopshire

---

* A series of easy-to-read children's books published by Random House.

5. *Are You My Mother?* by P. D. Eastman
6. *The Big Honey Hunt* by Stanley and Janice Berenstain
7. *Snow* by Roy McKie and P. D. Eastman

When one group of children is ready to start on a Beginner Book, the teacher must spend some time teaching the new words that have been compiled from each book, *before* the children read it. These new words are not taught as sight words to be remembered by their shape. The teacher shows the structure of these words by printing the letters in the customary fashion in red, blue, and gold. Soon these words will be incorporated in the child's reading vocabulary, so that he can read the books fluently and enjoy the content without having to stop and decipher new words.

The transition from the first Beginner Books to slightly harder children's books becomes easier as the reading vocabulary expands. Many children accomplish it in first grade. The choice of these books should depend completely on the interests of the individual child. Studies analyzing children's preferences in reading matter have shown that children of this age are chiefly interested in animals—imaginary or real. The second topic of greatest interest for children in the primary grades is reading about other children. When children have finished reading a book, the teacher should ask pertinent questions about the plot or a special character in the story. All outside reading can and should be used to practice the important reading skills which—as will be described in Chapter 9—are introduced early in the Structural Reading program.

In the second grade the words that have been casually introduced to facilitate outside reading in grade one will be systematically studied in structurally related groups. Here again, the child once more receives on an advanced level the thorough instruction which leads to the mastery of not only reading but also of writing the new groups of words.

At this point, individualized reading instruction has its most effective results. The necessary foundation for the whole class can be provided by worktexts D and E, which not only enlarge the reading and writing vocabulary but also carefully develop related reading skills and introduce the first grammatical concepts. From this background children should now branch out and read according to their interests and intelligence, instead of using a basal textbook.

Customarily, in second grade, children are still busy learning to read. In contrast, children taught by Structural Reading have progressed beyond this stage and can exercise their reading skills in areas such as science, social studies, and American history. They can and should read folktales, myths, legends, adventure stories, animal stories, humorous stories, biographies, and poetry.

The incentive to read comes first from the natural pleasure that stories give. It is closely followed by reading for information. Children who read with facility will be able to read to acquire factual knowledge. They will not need the excitement of a narrative to keep their attention while they struggle to decipher unfamiliar words. In Chapter 9 the development of the study skills is discussed in terms of teaching children to read comprehendingly the texts that the different school subjects require.

Reading "The cat ran" is the first step on the road to reading for pleasure and for the acquisition of knowledge; it smoothes the transition from the child's world of play to the world of letters. Almost no success in later life is as thoroughly enjoyed as the child's first realization that he can read a book. Two records illustrate the feeling of achievement that can fill a child who has just read his first book.

Jeff (6;0) read his first book with joy and pride. He opened it again as soon as he had finished it saying: "Now, I'm starting on the book again. I'll pretend I'm grown-up and you two are children, and I'll read to you."

When Tim (5;9) was given his first book, he read page after page spellbound, unable to stop. When he finished the book he danced through the room, exclaiming triumphantly: "I can read! I can read!"

Inculcating this attitude towards reading, this feeling for the pleasures of books, has been one of the most satisfactory results of Structural Reading instruction. Intellectual achievement and the enjoyment of books thus becomes a permanent part of the children's lives.

CHAPTER SEVEN

The Systematic Expansion of the Reading and Writing Vocabulary

" 'It's adding insult to injury,' said the parrot who was taken from his native land and forced to talk—in the English language." Sam Weller's complaint in *Pickwick Papers* describes equally well the plight of the child whose native tongue is English, and who is embarked on learning to read and write in it. Consider, for example, the following English words; they all end in *ow*, but they are pronounced in two different ways: *low* but *allow*, *know* but *now*, even *row* but *row*, and as every dog knows, *bow* but *bow* and *bow-wow*. Listening to these words, no child would ever be able to figure out that the vowel sounds in *low* and *allow* are recorded by the same letters, *ow*.

The child's plight is considerably lessened when the teaching of reading and spelling begins with phonetically regular words— those that have a one-to-one correspondence between sounds and letters—and only after these are mastered goes on to irregular words, which are also taught in structurally related groups.

Another way to lessen the inherent difficulties of English for the child is to avoid teaching reading and spelling separately, as is done in the sight method. With this method children learn to read by memorizing the appearance of a word, whereas they learn to spell by memorizing a sequence of letters. A child who is taught spelling in this fashion cannot benefit from the fact that so many words are structurally related—even in the highly irregular English language—that knowledge of the spelling of one word helps one learn the correct spelling of all related words. If a child learns to say to himself "dee yu cee key" when he wants to write *duck* and "dee yu es tee" for *dust,* the words seem as unrelated as the numbers 325 and 352.

If, on the other hand, the children gain insight into the structure of words, they are able to spell, as well as read, all related words, such as *duck, dust,* and *dull* by transfer.

Structural Reading teaches reading, writing, and spelling simultaneously, with the result that each of these language aspects sustains and reinforces the other. The speaking vocabulary is used as the point of departure for spelling, just as it was for reading. The child learns to read by listening to the spoken word first, and then he studies how it is recorded in print. The same sequence is followed in spelling, but now it is the child who says the word and, listening to himself, records the sounds he hears. Since the first words introduced are phonetically regular, he can write each word by this means, which we call self-dictation.

In the Structural Reading method the development of the vocabulary—listed by key words in the Teacher's Editions—is designed to give children a successful start and a broad foundation on which to build. As has been pointed out before, colored type is used in the Structural Reading Series to accentuate the structure of new words: the magic *e* is printed in gold, the variations of root words (prefixes, suffixes) in green, and silent letters in broken gray lines.

In the grade one program, study words are introduced in black —as a signal to both pupils and teachers that this word needs special attention. The teacher must not tell the children to remember how these words *look*—she must pronounce each black-lettered word clearly and write it on the board, emphasizing its special structural characteristics. This same procedure is to be used whenever a word is introduced that is either an exception to a rule or is employed in the text before it has appeared on a teaching page.

The same sequence of tasks is also followed to help the child to progress from reading to writing:

1. The child realizes that the spoken word *jump* is recorded by *ju* and *mp.*

2. The child selects the domino with *ju* and adds the domino with the ending *mp,* thus constructing by himself the word *jump* from its main part and its ending.

3. The child writes the word *jump* and discovers that the main word-part *ju* is recorded by the two letters *j* and *u.* He completes the word by writing the final consonant blend *mp.*

In Chapter 5 we presented records that showed the reading performance in slow motion; here we add only examples that show transfer or that illustrate how mastery in spelling is attained.

The record that follows shows five-year-olds building and writing words from self-dictation—not by memorizing a succession of letters. As they are selecting the proper dominoes, they often talk about what they are looking for. When they are actually writing, their attention is focused on the difficult art of forming the letters, and they hardly pause to talk.

Kathy (5;6)	*Built*	*Commented*
	hu m	You didn't teach me *hum,* but I can build it. You know: hum a tune.

Wendy (5;2)		
	ja m	I need a *m.** You know why. I want to build *jam,* so I need a *m.*

Wendy learned to read the *ĭ*-words by transfer. She then had no difficulty in learning to build them.

Wendy	*Built*	*Commented*
	pi ll	I said *pill* to myself, and so I looked for the *pi* first, and then for the *ll.*

I gave Wendy the dominoes and asked her to build as many words as she could. Wendy built: *fin, tip, fix, hill, dig.* Then she built a new word she had not been taught so far:

Wendy	*Built*	*Commented*
	bi g	I built big! You know, a big girl.

* In cases where letters are italicized, e.g. *m,* we refer to the written letter which in this method, throughout grade one, is always called by its sound-name, i.e. [m], not by its alphabet name.

Wendy (5;5) loved to play the folder game (see Chapter 11). She took my *fi* which I had placed on *fig* on my side of the folder: "Please Mrs. G. can I have it for my *fi ll,* because it's almost the end of my lesson."

Peter (5;8)	*Built*	*Commented*
	pi g	That's *pi* and now I need a *g.*
	mi x	I use it for *mix,* so I need an *x.*
	ri m	That's *ri* and I need it for *rim.* Now I'll get a *m.*
	* hi t	See, I know how to spell *hit.*
Peter (5;9)		
	lo t	a lot!
	lo	Should I do another *lot?* (I: Can you think of another word?) I can do *lock;* it must be a sharp [k] at the end.
	lo ck	I did a new word, because there wasn't anything else to build except lock!

Since reading and writing are taught together, not only does the writing of a word help the child recognize it more quickly, but, in addition, the reading of a written word helps to point to and correct spelling mistakes. Since the children read by sounding out, reading back the written word to themselves makes them aware of what they have put down. If the word they read is not the word they wanted to write, they know themselves that they have spelled the word wrongly. Here are four examples.

Wendy (5;2)	*Wrote*	*Read it back to herself*
	sap	Sap. Oh no, I want to write sip.
	sip	That's it, now it says sip.
Ann (5;5)		
	is	Oh, it should say *his.*
	his	There, I said it to myself [hi s], and now it is right.

---

* Not taught before.

Kathy (4;11)

| jm | Oh boy, I am a stupid mistaker. |
| jam | See, it says *jam* now. |

After the word is finished, the children must get used to reading back the word they have written. This early "proofreading" leads to the detection and correction of spelling mistakes. A child who had great trouble remembering how to form letters and was therefore apt to make absurd spelling mistakes showed that she could correct her errors by proofreading what she had written. (This child, Emily, is one of the case studies in Chapter 12.)

Emily (5;8)	*Wrote*	*Read it back to herself*
	Dab Dad	I don't want it to say *Dab,* I mean *d.*
	sib	No that says *sib.*
	sip	Okay, now it says *sip!*
	pib	I know why that's wrong. It says *pib.*
	pig	Now it says *pig.*

Since most writing pages offer samples of the words to be written, we provide a spelling test which one of the children called the "nothing page." The pictures are given, and the children have to write down the corresponding words.

To help the children to advance quickly to the reading of new words at sight, rhyming games are introduced. Recognizing the acoustic similarity between rhyming words not only speeds up fluent reading but also develops confident spelling. The teacher presents orally a group of mono-syllabic rhyming words. The children realize that two words rhyme if they sound alike, except for the beginning sound. They learn to find a rhyming word for any word given by the teacher: they will say, for instance, *sick* if the teacher says *pick.* They also learn to select from a miscellaneous group pairs of words that rhyme, as in the group *dog, cat, pig, rat, log, wig.* Having grasped that rhyming words are those that *sound* alike, the children now discover that they look alike too: the vowel and the end-consonant are identical.

At this level, reading from left to right is so firmly established that no harm is done if word endings are emphasized. This is different from teaching the *ick* or *at* family, asking the children to add *s* or *p* to the phonograms *ick* or *at*—a procedure which we deplore.

Once the children have been taken through monosyllabic words with the five short vowel sounds, the next step is to introduce monosyllabic words with the five short vowels ended or preceded by a consonant blend: *lamp, flag*. Of the two groups, the first is easier to learn, since *la mp* has a structure similar to *la p* and the two sounds at the end are easily heard if the word is pronounced slowly and distinctly.

Again, the new words are introduced on the spoken level. The teacher asks: What do I mean if I say [la mp]? After a short period of oral practice in putting the spoken parts together, the children learn to break similar words into parts by themselves. The usual steps then follow: the children find in their books how the spoken word *jump* is recorded; they build it with the dominoes and then write the word. Since the children grasp the structure of these words, they learn to read and spell them with great facility. The building of these words presents no difficulty, as evidenced by the children's own comments. (The first example is taken from the record of Tommy, whose detailed case study appears in Chapter 12.)

Tommy (6;9)	Built	Commented
	te nt	First a *te* and then you need a *n* and a *t*.
	la mp	*la* and then *m* and *p*.
	we ll	First a *we* and then an *ll*.
	ca mp	*ca* and then *m* and then *p*.
	gi ft	*gi, f* comes next, then *t*.
	ju mp	Let's see, here is a *ju*, I need the *m* and *p*.
	mi lk	*mi* and then *l* and then *k*.
	we st	*we* and then *st. West* that is. It means like way out West. I am going to California next year to visit my grandmother.

Willa (6;11)   *Wrote*   *Commented*

                bent   I thought I wouldn't hear the [n],
                                     but I did.

Another child read the words below although they had not
yet been taught:

Freddy (6;11)   *Read*   *Commented*

                te nt, tent   Mommy is going to get me one.

                lo st, lost   You are lost in the woods.

                hu nt, hunt   Hunt a big wild tiger!

                ra ft, raft   If a man is stuck on an island he
                                     builds a raft.

                la nd, land   Where you build and make every-
                                     thing and live your life.

                po nd, pond   Oh pond, with fish in it and where
                                     you have picnics.

                gi ft, gift   A present at birthdays or at Christ-
                                     mas.

                be nt, bent   You hammer something and get it
                                     bent.

                bu lb, bulb   What you light up in a house when
                                     it is pitch dark.

                sa nd, sand   You dig in the sand and make tun-
                                     nels.

In order to help the children advance quickly to reading such
words at sight and writing them instantly, rhyming sets are studied together (*fast, mast, past, last; hand, band, land, sand*). If
these words are analyzed and learned in sets, the reading or
writing of each single word contributes to the confident knowledge of how each word in the same group is read or spelled. (For
rhyming games, see Chapter 11.)

Among the words ending in a consonant blend is the group of
words ending with *ng*. It is not the first encounter the children
have had with words containing two letters that represent one
sound; they have already learned the *sh* of *ship* and the *th* in
this. The nasal sound [ng] in *ring* or *song*, however, does not

give any clue to the letters by which it is to be recorded. But here, too, building *ring* and *song* with the dominoes demonstrates the structure of these words and thus enables the children to read and write these words with understanding.

Tommy (6;9)	*Built*	*Commented*
	ri ng	The first sound you hear is [ri], then [ng].
	kin	Oh you need a *g*.
	king	[He pronounces *king* again.]

The next group (*ink, tank*) contains the nasal sound just studied in *ring*. But whereas the nasal sound in ring ends the word, the nasal sound in *ink* and *tank* is followed by a distinctly heard [k].

We add a few comments from our records that show how children figure out such new words with full understanding.

Wendy (5;10)	*Read*	*Commented*
	bang, gang	[Transfer] I never had these before.
	pink	That's easy.

While learning words that end in consonant blends is relatively easy, special care must be taken in teaching the reading and writing of words with initial consonant blends, such as *flag, clock, crib,* and many more pages are devoted to them. The main word-parts of these words are built from the consonant blend *fl* or *cl* or *cr* welded to the following vowel: *fla g, clo ck, cri b.* As always, these words are introduced on the spoken level.

To give variety to the oral introduction of new words, a story called *The Lost Ring* precedes the first teaching page in Book C. In some of the sentences a word is replaced by the picture of the corresponding object; thus the children will pronounce the words *dress, crib, clock, flag, clam, crab, flat* when they read the story without having to read the words themselves. The teacher now pronounces each word in turn, clearly enunciating the beginning consonant blend welded to the vowel-sound and instructing the children to break these words into their component parts by pronouncing main part and ending (*dre ss, cri b*).

The first teaching page on which these words appear complies with the usual organization. Following the oral introduction, the children will pronounce each word as they see the picture. They will find that the main word-part in the printed word below the picture is now recorded with three letters, the consonant blend and the vowel; to this main word-part the end-consonant is added in the customary way. The children prepare to write the new words in this lesson by building them with the dominoes *fla* and *g*, *fli* and *p*, and so on. When they proceed to the writing task at the bottom of the page, they know that the [fla] or [fli] is recorded by three separate letters.

Once the structure of words starting with consonant blends is clearly explained, the children soon learn to read this group of words with full comprehension, as the following excerpts show.

Freddy (7;1)	*Read*	*Commented*
	dru g, drug	A drug store is a place where you shop.
	tri p, trip	You trip over a stump.
	dro p, drop	It drops—it starts to rain.
	fla g, flag	Flag of the United States.
	clo ck, clock	It tells time.
	sto p, stop	You stop at a red light.
Freddy (7:4)		
	dri ft, drift	Drift in the water.
	cro ss, cross	How can you tell the difference? How can a person tell whether it is a cross on the church or if a person is cross?

The following examples show transfer. Even in this difficult group the children can build words they have never seen before.

Linda (5;8)	*Built*	*Commented*
	twi g	I can build it.
	smo ck	[Transfer—has never seen the word before] "That's a sharp [k] at the end, so I need *ck*.

Although many children find it difficult to write these words, they are able to correct their own mistakes by reading the words back to themselves.

PLATE 1

_____ Sam _____

Sam has a pack.

Dan has a cap.

Jack has a sack.

Ann has a fan.

Dad has ham.

PLATE 2

A cat.

A fat cat.

A fat cat sat.

A fat cat sat
at a rag bag.

PLATE 3

Can a dog live on a rock?
Can a hog live in a sock?
Can a cat live in a pot?
It can not. It can not.

Can a rat live in a pan?
Can an ox live in a can?
Can a cat live in a pot?
It can not. It can not.

PLATE 4

PLATE 5

Tommy (6;9)	Built	Commented
	fa	No, I want *flag*.
	flag	There, that says *flag*.
	shell	No, I want it to say *swell*. I need
	swell	*swe* and then *ll*.
	sift	Sift, no. I want *swift*. That's it,
	swift	*swift!* Swift means very fast.

After all the word groups with short vowel sounds have been studied, it is time to introduce the words with the long vowel sounds. It may be advisable for the teacher to review at this time the alphabet names of the letters that have been taught at the end of the readiness program.

Before any rule is taught, the children must meet these new words on the spoken level and learn to hear the new sounds without seeing how they are to be recorded. Using pictures, the teacher asks the children to pronounce the names of the objects she shows them, such as *cane, gate, lake, cake, rake.* The teacher then asks: What vowel sound did you hear in these words. It is the long-$\bar{a}$ sound, the alphabet name of the letter *a*.

To help the teacher in introducing these words on the spoken level two scenes appear on page 61 of Book C. A landscape is shown, once in summer and once in winter, and the objects in the picture all have names that belong to the long-vowel words. The teacher points out the *gate,* pronounces it clearly, and asks which vowel sound the children hear. The words *wade, cake, snake, lake, plate, flame* are illustrated in the pictures. Riddle games may follow in which the children must find the objects and enunciate the words themselves. "It rhymes with *lake* and children like to eat it" (*cake*).

On the next page the function of the magic *e* is dramatized. The children are fascinated to see the magician changing the word *can* into *cane* merely by attaching a "golden" *e* to the word *can.* (See Plate 7.) This magic *e* changes the short $\breve{a}$ of the word *can* to the long $\bar{a}$ of *cane* while the *e* itself keeps silent; it produces no sound at all. The magician leaves an indelible picture in the child's mind, making it almost impossible for him to forget that when there is a magic *e,* the preceding vowel sound is long. Printing the magic *e* in gold throughout the teaching pages of Books C and D reminds the child of its function.

Interestingly enough, by using the magic *e* new words with long vowels need not be introduced in isolated vowel groups. For the first time the children will learn a *rule* that applies to all words ending in the magic *e*. Whether the words contain the vowels *a,* or *i,* or *o,* or *u,* or *e,* the silent *e* at the end of a word means that the preceding vowel is pronounced as its alphabet name sounds.

Understanding of this rule allows for transfer: a great many new words can be figured out easily by the child. As an example, we quote from the record of Wendy who, after having studied the *ī*-words, glanced ahead in the book at the teaching page of the *ō*-words.

Wendy (6;0)	*Read*	*Commented*
	rose, nose, hose	I didn't guess them; I read them. [She laughed.] These are all rhyming words.

The following excerpts from our records point up how easily the new words are read with full comprehension.

Jeff (5;9)

	tame	I am wild, Timmy is tame, a deer is not so tame.
	make	Make a sentence.
	same	These are the same boxes.
	came	Daddy came back.

Jeff (5;10)

	Bill lit the fire.	I hope he does not burn himself.
	The wind lifts the kite.	I hope it does not break.

Freddy (6;6)

	prize	Something you get after a game.
	slide	You slide down the banister.
	wade	Billy's boat sailed across the lake, and we had to wade to get it.
	stare	I stare at the moon in the sky.

Again dominoes are used as an introduction to writing these new words. A separate domino presents the golden *e* and helps the child to think of its special role. The role of the magic *e* was so well grasped by one child that after he had built *can* with the dominoes, he added the golden *e,* saying: "And now I turn on the magic *e* and the word says *cane.*"

Linda (5;9)	*Built*	*Commented*
	cap and cape	You know why I want to build it, because I know it so well.
	pine	See, it's not hard for me. I can hear it.
Peter (5;11)	*Built*	*Commented*
	rage	[Built by transfer.] Look I built *rage,* like I'm in a terrible rage.
	kit	That says *kit.* Now I'll add the magic *e* and it says *kite.*
Peter (5;11)	*Read*	*Commented*
	have	There shouldn't be a magic *e* if it says *have.* [I explain about exceptions to rules.]

Wendy's record shows how the writing of the newly learned words is done with full comprehension of the role of the magic *e.* Wendy felt so confident that she wanted to work without any help and therefore asked to be allowed to cover up the words on top of the teaching pages.

Wendy (5;11)	*Wrote*	*Commented*
	cane	This would have a magic *e.* It makes the *a* long.
	gate	[Covers up words on top of page.] I won't copy it because I know the word.
	shak[?] shake	I have to put the magic *e* on so it will say *shake.*
	hole	I wrote it without peeking.
	tu tube	First, you have to write *tu,* right? Then the *b* and then the magic *e.* I like to cover up the words, so I can write them by myself.

| cut, cute | Cute! That's the word I want. This is what I do. I write the word and then I look if it has a magic *e*. *Cūte*—you need one. |

Learning the magic *e* words brings to a close the development of the Grade One vocabulary. Following similar procedures, the Grade Two vocabulary is presented in structurally related groups. The groups follow one another in a sequence of increasing difficulty.*

The sequence of the vocabulary has been established by careful experimentation in our teaching. Children tend to grasp the structure of some word groups more easily than that of others.

Throughout the Grade Two program the teacher must follow the customary teaching procedure in analyzing new groups of words. To give an example: the teacher must *not* allow the child to look at the *word* ball on page 19 of Book D and then tell him what the printed word says. As always, learning must start with the spoken word [ball] which is evoked from the child when he sees the picture of the ball. He will be interested in discovering how this spoken word is recorded and will be able to grasp the structure of all the words belonging to this group. Only then should the teacher bring out in the discussion that here the vowel *a* is neither short as in *can* nor long as in *cane*. It has a new sound, caused by the modifying effect of the following *ll*.

There are other groups of words in which consonants such as *l* and *r* and *ld* affect the vowel that precedes them (key words: *ball, cold, star, horse,* and *girl*). Although the teacher should know this linguistic rule, we have found that second-graders fare better if they learn each of these groups separately, since the rule is not as strikingly simple as that for the magic *e*. The following example shows how quickly children learn to spell these words. By now self-dictation has become a customary procedure, available to the children at every level of difficulty.

| Ann (6;9) | *Wrote* | *Commented* |
| | skirt | This is how you write *skirt*. I just know. I say it to myself. |

* The complete vocabulary for both grades 1 and 2 is listed at the end of the teacher's editions of the Structural Reading Series worktexts.

Second-grade pupils already know the effect of the silent, final *e* in words like *gate* and *pine*. They can now study the groups of words in which the magic *e* follows immediately after the vowel (key words: *bee, pie, hoe* and *due*); of these groups the *bee* group is probably the easiest. In the Structural Reading Series the second *e* is gold-colored to accentuate its magic *e* function.

Kathy (6;1) experienced no difficulty in studying the group of words in which the magic *e* followed the first *e*. "You see I know you spell *green* with two *e*'s. If it had only one *e* it would say grĕn." When she came to page 43 of Book D (see Fig. 7.1) she looked at the sentences and discovered that all but the first sentence began with a noun containing a double *ee*. She reprimanded the authors: "You all made a mistake. The sisters don't have a double *e*."

Children easily grasp the generalization that when there are two vowels together in a word the second vowel is silent, thus giving the first vowel its long sound. These groups of words are *read* easily (key words: *day, goat, tea, nail*). However, here we face the greatest difficulty in *spelling*. The child must remember that *meet* and *meat* are words that sound exactly alike but that are spelled differently.

Freddy (6;9) noticed this difficulty. When he wrote *scream*, he said: "You could just as well write it with two *e*'s."

Therefore, these groups of words are deliberately separated in the book insofar as it was possible.

Next the children will learn the sound of the diphthongs *ou* and *ow* as in *cloud* and *clown*. A few children will be ready to enjoy learning the philological fact that the name of the letter *w* (double *u*) indicates that it "doubles for u," that it can take the place of *u*. Therefore *ou* and *ow* are pronounced the same way. However, to help the children decide which of the two spellings is correct we group words containing the *ow* diphthong together in the following jingle (from page 119 of Book D).

The clown wore a crown
As he rode the cow to town.
But the clown lost his crown
When he flipped upside down.

Mix-Ups

My sisters are grazing.

The fleet is stinging the boy.

The cheese is landing now.

The sheep are mending socks.

The sheet has trucks on it.

The street is on the bed.

The bee is in the ice box.

Fix-Ups

The _____ are grazing.

The _____ is in the ice box.

The _____ is landing now.

My _____ are mending socks.

The _____ has trucks on it.

The _____ is on the bed.

The _____ is stinging the boy.

Fig. 7.1

The children we taught liked such jingles very much and asked for more. We have, therefore, written many jingles that help teach the spelling of certain groups of words.* The children often learn them by heart, and although their literary value is

---

* Several of these jingles are printed in the Teacher's Editions of Books D and E.

dubious we have found their value as mnemotechnical devices to be undeniable.

The introduction of words containing silent letters that have no visible function makes children aware of the phonetic irregularities of the English language (key words: *lamb, knot* and *night*). Printing these silent letters in broken gray lines depicts the soundlessness of these letters and accentuates the structure of the word.

It is of great importance that only the correct spelling of a word should come before the child's eyes. It is a grave mistake to give spelling tests where the children have to decide whether a certain printed word is spelled correctly or wrongly. Spelling tests should be tests in which the teacher says a word and the child writes the word from self-dictation.

It is a pity that brand names which the child sees everywhere —in the kitchen, on T.V., or in subways and buses—are spelled incorrectly; the wrong spelling gets mixed with the right one.

The three vocabularies that the child has at his command each have a different scope. His speaking vocabulary is the most comprehensive, his reading vocabulary is next, and his writing vocabulary is least.

In teaching by the Structural Reading method, care is taken to increase all three. The speaking vocabulary grows as the teacher utilizes pictures, tasks, poems, and stories. The reading vocabulary follows closely.* The greatest difference between our method and others is the expansion of the writing vocabulary. So often a child is handicapped in writing compositions by the difficulties of spelling the words he wants to use. The simultaneous teaching of reading and writing in Structural Reading equips the child to express his thoughts adequately by being able to write with almost the same facility as that with which he speaks.

In the beginning the child should ask the teacher for help with the spelling of unfamiliar words. But dictionary skills are developed early, so the child can soon use the dictionary to help himself to spelling whatever unfamiliar words he wants to write.

The following story was written by Kathy (age six), working

---

* See the word lists at the end of the teacher's editions of the Structural Reading Series worktexts for the reading vocabulary of children taught by this method.

in a room by herself, who came to the teacher only to ask for the spelling of *everything, police, while, afterwards,* and *sheets.* She worked with an eraser and corrected herself, but since she wrote in another room no further help by grown-ups was given (see Fig. 7.2).

SNOW BALL

Once upon a time there was a little kitten named Snow Ball. She was my kitten and she was a good little kitten. One morning I could not find Snow Ball. I asked my Mother. She said: "Oh dear! I don't know where she is. We better start looking for her." We looked under everything we could think of. At last we called the police. A little while afterwards my Mother did my bed. When she got to the sheets what did she see but SNOW BALL!

THE END

Fig. 7.2

CHAPTER EIGHT

From the Spoken Word to Spelling Rules and the First Grammatical Concepts

No human being learns his native tongue by the rules of grammar. The child talks first, and learns the rules of his language considerably later. By the time he is six, a child knows that one speaks of one dog but many dog*s;* he says, "Look at me. I am jumping!" or "I jumped as far as I could in gym today," without knowing at all that he is speaking grammatically. He can speak correctly without conscious knowledge of the inner workings of English, but sooner or later he will need guidance for the understanding of the general principles, such as the formation of plurals or the inflection of root words, that are necessary for correct spelling and the development of the first grammatical concepts.

Children must grasp that what they say spontaneously does not apply to this word or that only, but that there are rules that hold true generally. Attention is first drawn to the fact that in the spoken language special changes regularly occur that must similarly be observed in writing. These changes are governed by rules which the child will discover, grasp, and apply.

It is essential for teachers to understand fully that it is not only possible but imperative to help children grasp rules intuitively, prior to the verbal formulation of those rules. To ˙ ?ach the rule first, before it is understood, means that it can only be learned by memorization; such recitation does not ensure insight into the structural characteristics underlying the rule.

Children must first get a sense of the essence of a rule and understand how it works. They will show their understanding by applying it correctly, many of them with delight, because they know what to do in a new case without having to be told. These concrete experiences prepare for the later understanding of an exact statement of the rule. Helping the children understand the rule before teaching its verbalization prepares them to grasp it maturely when it is introduced. This practice is in accordance with Jerome S. Bruner's stress on the same approach in the teaching of mathematics: "For . . . it may be of the first importance to establish an intuitive understanding of materials before we expose our students to more traditional and formal methods of deduction and proof." [1]

In Structural Reading intuitive understanding is achieved with the help of functional drawings. The first rule that the pupils grasp in this way concerns the function of the magic *e*. Prior to the introduction of the magic *e*, pictures in the worktexts have no other purpose but that of a picture dictionary; they supply the child with a spoken word, which he finds recorded under each picture. Beginning with the introduction of the magic *e*, the pictures illustrate a rule the child has to grasp. The golden *e* reminds the child that the *e* at the end of words like *lake, cube,* and *slide* has a magic quality: it keeps silent but makes the preceding vowel say its alphabet name. As shown in Chapter 7, our case records prove that children can apply this rule effectively not only in reading but in spelling as well. Interestingly enough, they are often able to formulate rules in their own words.

As we describe the ongoing steps in teaching by the Structural Reading method, the consistency of our method will become evident. In Structural Reading teaching always starts on the oral level, where the child is guided by his own usage of words and word forms. This is followed by the study of functional illustrations. This, in turn, is followed by tasks in which the rule just learned is applied, testing the child's mastery of it.

The first rule treated in this fashion is the formation of plurals. Every child knows the difference between the singular and the plural. He likes to be given one piece of candy and likes even better to get several pieces. From his knowledge of oral forms he must advance to the grammatical rule governing the formation of plurals. As always, the teacher introduces the new concept on the spoken level, displaying a picture of one dog and another with several dogs, or one doll and then many dolls. As the teacher points to one dog, the pupil will pronounce the word *dog;* as she points to several dogs, the child will hear himself say, dog*s*. He will hear the same difference between doll and doll*s*, and discover that in each case a final *s,* added to the singular form *dog* or *doll,* indicates that there is more than one dog or doll. Because in every case the children hear the ending *s* clearly, and because this ending is attached to words they have already studied, they can often read as well as write plurals without any difficulty. Some children, indeed, have read the page on which plurals are introduced (page 3 of Book C) without any help; analyzing the page, they were able to formulate the rule of how to form plurals on their own.

Kathy (5;6) read the page without any help.

Read		*Commented*
1 doll	2 dolls	There are more than one!
1 dog	3 dogs	

Kathy turned to me disappointedly: "Oh, I hoped we'd learn something new."

Reads *leg* on the word lotto card. "But on the picture there are two legs and it says *leg,* so you should have only one leg in the picture."

Tommy (6;9) working on page 3 commented: "You put an *s* there because you want to say dolls. There is more than one."

The children are not expected to be able to formulate the rule: to form plurals, in most cases, an *s* is added to the word standing for one object. At this level it is enough that the concept is grasped, and that the rule is correctly applied.

In second grade, the children will discover the more complicated formation of plurals of words ending in *s, ss, sh, z, zz, ch,* and *x*. As the children hear themselves say, dress*es,* branch*es,* or fox*es,* they gain a feeling for the necessity of these language forms. Experimentation on the spoken level will show that it is hard for anyone to add an *s* to a word like *dress* or *witch* or *fish* since their singular form already ends with a similar sound. A functional drawing on page 16 of Book D explains what is done in these cases: we add the two letters *es* to form the plurals of words ending in *s, ss, sh, z, zz, ch,* and *x.*

The formation of plurals ending in *y* is deferred until after the general rule about changing *y* to *i* in the middle of a word has been studied.

Parallel to the rules about the addition of *s* to form plurals of nouns are the rules for forming the present tense of a verb in the third person singular. (Prior to this the children have learned the use of pronouns.) The children will spontaneously say: "Let us run!" and "Ann runs," and the teacher must simply direct their attention to their own usage. It is easy for even the first-grade child to grasp that if a third person—not *I, you, we,* or *they,* but Ann, John, Dad, Mother or any single person—performs an action then *s* is added to the action word. If the concept is clear, reading and writing "Ann sit*s* still, John run*s* home, Dad step*s* on the truck, Mother sing*s* a song" will be done correctly. When the child does make a mistake he often corrects his written work when he reads it back to himself.

Ann (6;2) wrote "Dad dig." She read it back to herself. "Oh, but I want to say Dad digs. I must put an *s* on dig."

The more difficult cases of writing the present tense in the third person singular of verbs ending in *zz, sh, ss, ch,* and *x* is studied in second grade. Let the children now say what Bob does if he tries to catch fish. It is impossible to add an *s* to a word that ends in a similar sound. The child will hear himself say, "Bob catch*es* a fish," thus discovering that he adds *es* to catch just as he did when forming the plurals of nouns with the same endings. Whereas we add an *s* to *run* in the third person singular, we add *es* to *rush* or *catch:* he rush*es* or catch*es.* On each teaching page of Book D there are tasks that demand that the pupil apply what the rule has taught him, and there are many tests in ensuing stories that will show the teacher whether or not the rule is not only understood but correctly applied.

The following record clearly shows that a child taught in this way understands the reasoning underlying the rule; using her own words Ann is able to explain her actions in each instance.

Ann (7;4)	Formed the plural	Commented
	matches	When you have two matches you can't say [matchs]. When you have to write them, you don't just put an *s*, you put *es*.
	rushes	You can't say [rushs] because the [sh] sounds a lot like the [s] sound, so you need to have an *es*.
	tosses	Because if you just add an *s* it would just be [toss].
	catches	*Catchs* would be too hard to say; *catches* is easier to say.
	fixes	In that word the *x* sounds like the *s*. If you just add the *s*, you can't hear it; so you add *es*.
	washes	Because the *sh* sounds like *s*.
	mops	That time they put a plain, ordinary *s* because [p] is so different from the [s] sound, so you can say "Dad mops."

After Ann had studied pages 16 and 17 of Book D she took a test —printed below—which she completed with utter confidence.

TEST

Let us run!	*Mary* runs.
Let us catch fish!	*Bob* catches *fish.*
Let us toss the ball!	*Bill* tosses *the ball.*
Let us sing!	*Ann* sings *a lovely song.*
Let us wash our hands!	*Dick* washes *his hands.*

As in the case of pluralization of nouns, the child will learn to read and write the third person singular of verbs like *cry, fly, dry* after the rule of changing *y* to *i* is fully understood.

Another instance that shows once again how children, because they handle spoken words accurately, can easily learn the general rule needed for correct writing is the formation of the possessive and the use of the apostrophe. The children know what it means to say, "This is Jack's book," but they must discover that in writing, the *s* they hear in Jack's book is preceded by a new symbol, the apostrophe. To show the necessity of using the apostrophe the teacher should write *mothers* on the board and explain that "mothers" have "aprons" *sounds* exactly like "mother's aprons." Without the apostrophe, the written word *mothers* would be mistaken for a plural form. To give practice in this new concept the teacher should tell the children to condense the following sentences into two words: "This apron belongs to Mother" (Mother's apron). "This car is owned by Dad" (Dad's car). "This ball is one of the toys of Kathy's" (Kathy's ball). The children comprehend that the object mentioned is something that belongs to someone, something that someone possesses; they will be ready later to understand the term *possessive* that is given to this form.

How well six-year-old children comprehend this new concept is illustrated by the following comments:

Wendy (6;2) read page 48 of Book C without any instruction: " 'This is Jack's bat.' That means that the bat is his."

Emily (6;4) commented: "You put the new sign there. That means it belongs to the person. Here the dress belongs to Jill."

"I put the new sign there because that means the top belongs to Bill. This way it is shorter."

Immediately after Emily finished page 48 of Book C, she completed the test printed below with complete confidence in 8 minutes.

TEST

This is Bill. Bill has a top.
This is <u>Bill's</u> *top.*

This is Ann. Ann has a doll.
This is <u>Ann's</u> *doll.*

This is Jim. Jim has a dog.
This is <u>Jim's</u> *dog.*

This is Fred. Fred has a desk.
This is <u>Fred's</u> *desk.*

Towards the end of second grade, the children learn another function of the apostrophe—its use in contractions to indicate a missing letter. Simple contractions, such as *don't* for the two words *do* and *not,* are made clear by a structural explanation enabling children to grasp the concept and to spell the contractions correctly, marking the omission by an apostrophe each time.

Willa (6;5) said "I put an apostrophe in *I'm,* because I took away a letter."

In contrast, children who come for remedial help make mistakes that show that they have not understood the function of the apostrophe.

Todd (8;10) wrote *your* for *you are, lets* for *let us* and *shes* for *she is.* After being taught pages 52 ff, he formed these contractions correctly. As he wrote *let's* he commented: "I dropped the *u,* so I put an apostrophe in its place to show that the *u* is gone."

One of the most important concepts children learn in second grade is the inflection of root words. Here, too, the teacher must never dictate a rule to be memorized. Children must be guided by their own natural use of word forms; the pronunciation of a spoken word indicates what the printed and written word must *say.* Functional drawings on the teaching page lead the children to the discovery of the general rule.

The teacher introduces the present participle by writing words like *stand, lift,* and *sing* on the board. We say, "Bill should *stand* up." If he is doing it now, we say, "Bill is _____ up." The pupils will readily supply the correct form, *standing.* After more of these examples, the children grasp the fact that they use the ending *ing* if they talk about an action that is being done at the present moment. The functional drawing on page 39 of Book D (see Plate 8) shows how these words are recorded: the ending *ing* printed in green letters, is added to the root word. The written word corresponds to the pronunciation of the spoken word. The children use this new knowledge to write the words. By the end of page 39 they are able to understand the jingle giving the rule for *all* words of a similar structure.

> *To make bend into bending.*
> *call into calling, or mend into mending,*
> *fall into falling, or spend into spending,*
> *you always need the very same ending.*
> *What do you need?* _____

Our records show that without exception the children can supply the ending *ing* to answer this question.

The addition of the ending *ing* to the root word is only adequate when dealing with monosyllabic verbs that end in two consonants. The formation of the present participle of verbs ending in magic *e* is slightly more complex. Forming the participle on the spoken level presents no difficulty; there is no difficulty in pronouncing *baking, wading, riding, joking,* etc., correctly. However, in writing the participle an obstacle presents itself. We can't add *ing* to *bake;* it would look like bakeing and would be pronounced incorrectly. What do we have to do? Plate 9 (from page 41 of Book D) indicates the proper procedure: the magic *e* must be dropped before the ending *ing* is added.

The third case to be studied in the formation of the present participle comprises monosyllabic verbs ending in one consonant. The teacher should ask what a driver is doing in front of a red light. The answer will undoubtedly be that the driver is *stopping* the car. On the oral level, the sound of the root word *stop* is not altered when the ending *ing* follows it. But how do we write *stopping?* If we follow the first impulse, we would add *ing* to *stop;* it would look like *stoping* and read as if stop had the long vowel sound instead of its short one. If we try it with *hop,* the word *hoping* would even have another meaning: it would mean someone is hoping for something to happen, and not that he is hopping. Something must be done before we add *ing* to root words like *stop* or *hop* so that the present participle lets us hear the same vowel sound that is heard in the root words *stop* and *hop:* the short sound of [o]. The picture on page 47 of Book D (see Plate 10) demonstrates that before the ending *ing,* printed in green letters, is added, the end consonant must be doubled. This holds true for all verbs in which the short vowel-sound is followed by one consonant only. The doubling must be done to keep the vowel short.

The inflection of root words makes sense since they follow one general idea clearly expressed in speech. The ending *ing* must be added in such a way that the pronunciation of the root word is never altered. This general idea guides the special rules for each of the three cases listed below.

1. Verbs ending in two consonants preserve the short vowel

even if *ing* is added to the root. To these verbs (*mend, mending*) the ending *ing* is added without any variation.

2. Verbs ending in magic *e* would not be correctly pronounced if *ing* were to be added directly. The *e* must be dropped before *ing* is added: *bake, baking.*

3. Verbs ending in one consonant would be mispronounced if *ing* were to be added directly to the root word. This is prevented by doubling the consonant: *hop, hopping.*

Once the structural characteristics of these three cases are grasped, children have no difficulty in applying the rules to the formation of the past tense, when they add *ed,* or to the formation of a noun from the verb form, where they add *er* (mend*ed,* bak*ed,* shopp*ed;* hunt*er,* div*er,* sitt*er*). The same principle holds true when the children add *y* to create an adjective from a noun or when they add *er* or *est* to the root word to form the comparative (sand*y,* shak*y,* mudd*y;* tall*er,* tall*est,* fin*er,* fin*est,* bigg*er,* bigg*est.*)

Children who have been taught to understand the structural characteristics of all three cases have no trouble applying the rule, as the following example shows:

Wendy (6;5)	*Wrote*	*Commented*
	baker	Oh, I have to drop the magic *e.* You have to drop *e* when you add *er.* You can't have two *e*'s. It wouldn't say *baker.*

In contrast, consider the difficulties of two students who came to us for remedial help in reading:

Jim (8;7), a very bright third grader, said, "I have a problem. I don't know when to double and when to drop something." After having studied the functional drawings illustrating the three cases in Book D, Jim was able to complete the written exercises without help.

Todd (8;10) was equally uncertain. He said, "I've forgotten when you double."

After studying the three cases in Book D, Todd was given the test reprinted below. He completed it without hesitation.

TEST

	HE IS DOING IT NOW	HE DID IT IN THE PAST
to step	stepping	stepped
to mend	mending	mended
to stop	stopping	stopped
to bake	baking	baked
to rob	robbing	robbed

Some children point out that we do not drop the *e* when we write bak*ed* and bak*er;* they say that here the *d* and *r* are simply added to the verb *bake.* But the rule of dropping the magic *e* must be preserved, especially since it is important in the later study of syllabication. In syllabication the division always occurs between root word and the inflectional ending. We say ba/king, but we must divide bak-ing, bak-ed, bak-er. In these written word forms we clearly see the root (bak-) deprived of the magic *e,* before the inflectional ending is added.

For children who learn by the Structural Reading method the study of words with prefixes or suffixes presents no difficulty. Children begin by breaking the word *apart* into the two parts they hear distinctly, *a* and *part.* The teacher should explain that *a* is called a prefix; that a prefix is a syllable at the beginning of a word that usually changes the word's meaning. Actually, of course, the syllable *pre* is itself a prefix. It means *before* or *ahead of,* and we hear it at the beginning of many words: *pre*view, *pre*dict, *pre*fer.

The study of suffixes proceeds in the same way and is equally intelligible to the child. Functional drawings are used to show that a prefix or a suffix is simply added to the root word without changing the root spelling. The prefix or suffix, however, is sometimes altered, as when the *l* from *all* is omitted in words such as *altogether,* and the second *l* of *full* is omitted in words like *hopeful* or *harmful.*

These words present no special problems; moreover, here is a fine opportunity for raising interesting questions about the English language. For example, if someone is *up*set or *up*sets a table, the prefix *up* is combined with the word *set* to describe a mishap. But when we set up a badminton net, this is a constructive and not a destructive action.

Whenever possible, the meaning of a prefix or a suffix should be explained. Children are interested to hear that the prefixes *un* and *re* have special functions derived from their use in Latin. The prefix *un* means *not,* as seen in *untie* or *unfold;* it describes the opposite of the root *tie* or *fold.* The prefix *re* means back or again: the words *return, recall,* and *replace* mean turn back, call back to mind, and put back in place, respectively.

The following excerpt shows how thoroughly a child can understand the meaning of the prefix *un.*

After Ann (7;4) had studied the prefixes in the worktext I gave her the following test.

I: Your mother is kind, but there are people who are not. What are they ?

Ann: Unkind.

I: What does *unlatch* mean?

Ann: Somebody had latched the door and later he unlatched it.

I: What does *unlucky* mean?

Ann: I was not lucky in playing the Barbie Game.

As Ann studied the suffix *ful,* she commented on several of the words:

Ann (7;4)	*Read*	*Commented*
	handful	If you have some peanuts and Mommy says you can only take a handful.
	thankful	That's like at Thanksgiving, you are very thankful.
	careful	. . . means if you do something, you should be careful—you just take care.

As the children progress from the monosyllabic words to the reading and writing of words of more than one syllable, it is of great help to be able to divide such words into syllables. The child uses words like *hammer, paper,* or *animal* in his speech with ease, but when he meets such words for the first time in print, they present some difficulties. If the child has learned to divide them into syllables, he finds them easy to decipher. The same is true in writing; the child must dictate syllable after syllable to himself to be able to write polysyllabic words down with confidence. If the child dictates the word *mending* or *animal* to himself, he would say men/ding or a/ni/mal, which is his natural pronunciation of these words, and will spell them correctly.

Unfortunately, syllabication, that is, the correct division of words into syllables, has rules of its own which often do not conform with the natural division of syllables in speech. It is possible, however, to avoid any mention of this disparity, and to preserve the idea that the spoken word is our guide without misinforming the children. We can now teach two major rules which interest children and enable them to grasp the structural principle. Of course, this must be done with a minimum of technical language but in the most precise manner.

Syllabication has a practical use that children can understand: when a writer finds no room at the end of a line to write an entire word, he must know where to divide it. For the second-grade pupil, it is enough to understand the structural characteristics of two major groups of words. The first group is one in which grammar has priority over pronunciation. In the second, division into syllables depends on the pronunciation of the vowel in the first syllable, that is, whether the vowel is long or short.

The first group governs three cases: where there is an inflection of a root word, where a prefix precedes the root, and where a suffix follows the root. In all these instances, *the root must emerge unscathed:* the division must be made between root and inflectional ending (mend-ing), between prefix and root word (re-turn), between root and suffix (help-less). We *say* men-ding but we divide mend-ing. We say ba/ker, but we divide: bak-er. Syllabication explains, moreover, a difficult point in an earlier lesson. As we said, we do not change *bake* to *baker* or *baked* by adding *r* or *d* to the root. When *bak-* appears at the end of a line, separated from the ending *ing* or *er* or *ed,* it becomes clear that the *e* has been dropped before any of these endings are attached.

In this first group there is one special point to be emphasized: verbs like *run, stop,* and *hit* double the consonant before the inflectional endings are added, in order to keep the vowel short. This added consonant belongs to the second syllable: actually we add *ning* to *run, ping* to *stop, ting* to *hit* (run-ning, stop-ping, hit-ting). The same holds true for the related forms, stop-ped, stop-per, and so on.

Although children in second grade do not ordinarily learn rules about syllabication, it makes later study easier if they get a feeling for the main principles at this stage. First, the child should review how he added *ing* to *mend* to form *mending*. Now it can be pointed out that the separation into syllables follows exactly the same pattern; we separate *mending* into *mend-* and *ing*.

Willa (8;2) was shown pages 39 ff. in Book D and was then given the test printed below, in which she had to divide given words. There was only room on each line to write part of each word, so that dividing the word was required and seemed natural.

TEST

sending; ing	send-	*started;* ed	start-
riding; ing	rid-	*diver;* er	div-
dropping; ping	drop-	*printer;* er	print-
filled; ed	fill-	*drummer;* mer	drum-
skated; ed	skat-	*rosy;* y	ros-

Not only did she divide all the words correctly, but her comments show how well she understood the task. (She completed the test in five minutes.)

Willa (8;2)	*Read*	*Commented*
	sending	I get it. You write only *send-,* and you put the *ing* on the new line.
	dropping	You put only *drop-* on one line and then *ping* on the next line.
	filled	You put *fill-* on one line. On the next line you put *ed.*
	skated	You put *skat-,* drop the magic *e,* and then you put *ed* on the next line.

> You separate just the way you put
> it together. You have *skate*—you
> drop the *e* and then add *ed*.

The second major group of words follows one clear principle —the preservation of pronunciation. The words in this group must be divided so that the first syllable indicates whether the vowel is short or long, that is, whether there is a closed syllable, as in *bas-ket,* in which the vowel is fenced in between two consonants, or an open syllable, as in *ba-sis,* in which the vowel is long. To keep the vowel short we fence it in between two consonants; to keep it long, it must stand alone.

The first words in this group to be studied are those with a double consonant in the middle. The teacher should have a pupil pronounce such words, one after another: *ladder, supper, butter.* As the child listens to these words he easily hears the syllable division into *lad-der, sup-per,* and *but-ter.* The teacher should write *ladder* on the board and point out that it is separated into *lad-der* to show the pronunciation of the short vowel in the first syllable. Functional drawings again help in making the separation of the words into syllables clear: for example, two horses pull the word *lad-der* apart.

In many words the short vowel sound in the first syllable is followed not by a double-consonant but by two different ones, as in *basket, number, napkin.* But as before, these words are divided first on the oral level and then in reading and writing into *bas-ket, num-ber, nap-kin.* The vowel in the first syllable must be fenced in by two consonants to preserve its short sound.

Digraphs such as *th* or *ck* are not counted as two consonants since they represent but *one* sound. If they follow a short vowel, they are assigned to the first syllable: *moth-er, tick-et.* Suppose there is no room at the end of the line and the word *mother* has to be divided. If we see *mo-,* we would pronounce it with the long vowel, since it is an open syllable. Instead, if we see *moth-* we know the vowel is short. So it makes sense to divide *moth-er,* but *fa-ther.*

In the next section words are studied in which the first vowel has a long sound in the first syllable, and is followed by only one consonant. As the children hear the words *paper, spider, demon,* they have no trouble pronouncing them in syllables: *pa-per, spi-der, de-mon.* To preserve the long sound of the vowel in the first syllable, the vowel must stand alone at the end of the syllable. If the consonant that follows were assigned to the first syllable, the vowel would be wrongly pronounced as a short sound (*pap-er*). Thus the rule makes sense; in a word of two syllables, *in which the first vowel sound is long,* the one consonant that follows is assigned to the second syllable.

It is interesting that the division into syllables of words that differ only in their initial sounds, such as in *lemon* and *demon,* must be divided differently. To preserve the short vowel in the first syllable of *lemon* we separate *lem-on;* to preserve the long vowel in the first syllable of *demon* we separate *de-mon.* The same is true with related words like *Eliz-a-beth* and *Eli-za* or with similarly spelled words like *min-ute* and *mi-nus, mis-ery* and *mi-ser.* In each case the pronunciation of the vowel determines the syllabication.

The teaching of syllabication progresses easily from two-syllable words to those of three syllables. Words like *holiday* and *president* fall naturally into the groups which were governed by the rules for two-syllable words (*hol-i-day, pres-i-dent, yes-ter-day*).

The following record shows how easily a child in second grade grasped the explanation—given in simple terms—of the rules governing long and short vowel sounds. Again we prepared a test (see below). Kathy (7;9) completed it without a single mistake and with complete confidence.

TEST

letter	let-	*sister*	sis-
ter		ter	
dinner	din-	*open*	o-
ner		pen	
spider	spi-	*doctor*	doc-
der		tor	
whisper	whis-	*cider*	ci-
per		der	
music	mu-	*gallop*	gal-
sic		lop	
hammer	ham-	*druggist*	drug-
mer		gist	

Her comments showed that she understood the reasoning behind the rules.

Kathy (7;9)	*Read*	*Commented*
	letter	Well, you have *lĕt* not *lē*, so I write *let;* all that is left is *ter* for the next line.
	dinner	You have to write *dĭn*, not *dī*, so I separate after *dĭn*.
	spider	It has to be *spī*, not *spĭd*, so I separate after *spī*.
	whisper	It has to be *whĭs*, not *whī*, so I divide the word after *whĭs*.
	music	It has to be *mū* not *mŭs*.
	hammer	It has to be *hăm*, not *hā*, so I divided it there.
	sister	It has to be *sĭs*, not *sī*, so you divide it there.
	open	It has to be *ō*, not *ŏp*, so you divide it after *ō*.
	doctor	It has to be *dŏc*, not *dō*.
	cider	It has to be *cī*, not *cĭd*.
	* gallop	It has to be *gal*, not *gā*.
	* druggist	It has to be *drug*, not *drū*.

With equal ease, Kathy was able to draw a line through printed words in the worktext to show how each word should be divided into syllables. She even correctly separated words that have a digraph in the middle, such as "moth-er" and "weath-er."

From the above record we can see how a seven-year-old grasps a rule and expresses it in simple terms that show that she understands what she is doing. Remedial students, on the other hand, have often come to us for help, confused although they had memorized their teachers' formulation of the rules.

To point out that the verbalization of a rule does not lead to insight we have chosen a record of a remedial student as an illustration of the next topic taught.

Todd (8;10) only vaguely knew when *y* had to be changed to *i*, but since he did not understand the rule, he did not feel confident about applying it. "I can never remember when to put an *i* and a *y*."

---

* Words that had not been studied before.

Some words and sentences dictated to Todd are reproduced below.

DICTATION

candy   candys
Lets give it a try.
He trys very hard.

To demonstrate the underlying generalization, three cases with the same structural characteristics are presented. The functional drawings and the poem on page 76 of Book E (see Fig. 8.1) helped Todd to understand the general principle; the final *y* must be changed to *i* in the middle of a word. Printing the *y* of eas*y* and the *i* in eas*i*ly below each other effectively accentuates the rule governing the change. In all adjectives ending in *y*, *y* changes to *i* when the adverb is formed by adding *ly* to the adjective (luck*y*-luck*i*ly; happ*y*, happ*i*ly).

On page 77 of Book E (see Fig. 8.2) Todd studied nouns ending in *y*. In this case, the *y* is changed to *i* when the plural is formed (pupp*y*, pupp*i*es). The plural formation includes adding *es* instead of *s*. This is another instance where the plural is formed by adding *es* (see *match-matches*). The illustration on page 78 of Book E (see Fig. 8.3) shows that similarly, in verbs ending in *y*, not only is the *y* changed to *i* in the third person singular but the ending *es* is added instead of a single *s* (dr*y*, dr*ies*). Likewise, to form the past tense the *y* is changed to *i* before the *ed* is added (dry, dr*ied*).

Instead of repeating the rule blindly, Todd was able to deduce from the functional drawings the consistent behavior of Mr. Y. His thorough understanding of this rule is evident in his remarks after he had studied pages 76, 77 and 78 of Book E.

Todd (8;10) said "Oh yes, I get it. . . . For instance, when you are talking about he or she *tries,* you change the *y* to *i* and put *es* at the end. You don't have a *y* in the middle of a word."

In the test he now took he made no mistakes.

DICTATION

candy   candies
Let's give it a try.
He tries very hard.

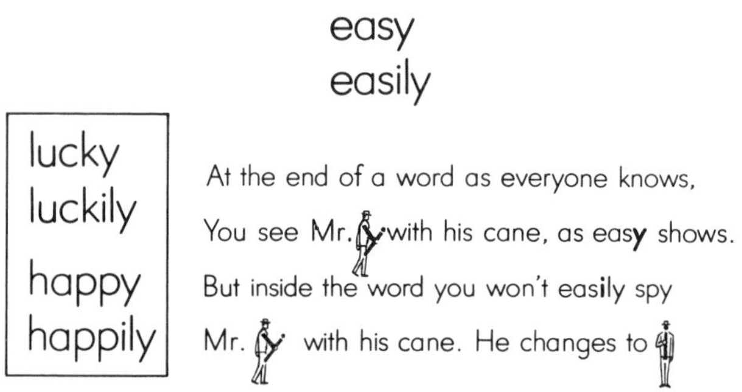

easy
easily

lucky
luckily

happy
happily

At the end of a word as everyone knows,

You see Mr. Y with his cane, as eas**y** shows.

But inside the word you won't eas**i**ly spy

Mr. Y with his cane. He changes to i

Fig. 8.1

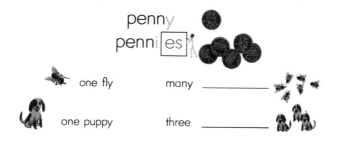

penny
penni es

one fly   many _____

one puppy   three _____

Fig. 8.2

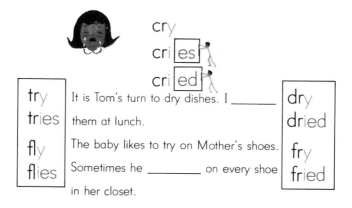

cry
cri es
cri ed

try
tries
fly
flies

It is Tom's turn to dry dishes. I _____
them at lunch.

The baby likes to try on Mother's shoes.
Sometimes he _____ on every shoe
in her closet.

dry
dried
fry
fried

Fig. 8.3

Although syntax as such is not taught in first and second grade, the children are led to experiment on their own level with concepts that will later be deepened. For instance, in Book B, in the first grade, the children learn to distinguish on the spoken level between a statement and a question, and thus understand the function of the period and the question mark. They learn to use the correct punctuation in writing, to indicate with punctuation the difference between a written statement or a question. Later in second grade, the children grasp, with the same facility, that a sentence presents a complete thought, but a phrase gives only a part of a thought.

It is not important that children in second grade learn technical terms. However, in preparation for later detailed study of the parts of speech, they should learn that *each word in a sentence has a definite function*. As early as Book B, when studying the words *ran* and *sat* the children learned that these words are different from previously learned words. Up till then, the words described an object or a person; these new words are action words, describing something that is happening.

On page 3 of Book D children are asked to choose the proper adjective to fit a given noun and to reject the two that would not fit; they learn in this exercise that an adjective is a word that describes or modifies a noun. On page 74 of Book E they find that adding *ly* to an adjective makes it into an adverb. From studying the effect of these words, children are prepared to understand that this set of words describes or modifies verbs.

As early as first grade we introduce special tasks to help children develop a feeling for the different roles that various parts of speech play in a sentence. Mix-Ups and Fix-Ups serve as excellent preparation for the later study of technical terms as well as for the diagramming of a sentence. In the Mix-Ups, children are presented with a few sentences; each sentence, for one reason or another, is absurd as it stands. The proper subject of one sentence may have been exchanged with that of another sentence, as on page 85 of Book D (see Plate 11). To fix these Mix-Ups, the children must read each sentence judiciously until they find its proper subject. This task is repeated often in the Structural Reading worktexts using predicates and objects as well as mixed-up subjects.

The Mix-Ups strike the children as funny, and they like to

hunt for the word that would make sense in the context. They quickly glance over the worktext page, looking for the *part of speech* in each sentence which they need for the Fix-Ups. In each case, they learn to examine only the subjects, or only the predicates, or only the objects of the given sentences.

Willa (6;7) came to a Mix-Up page (page 68 of Book D) and exclaimed: "I know that kind—they come out all right in the end!"

Thus, this favorite task in the worktexts prepares children for the understanding of a complex study that is so often difficult—the diagramming of a sentence.

Throughout this chapter we have shown that instruction in Structural Reading relies primarily on children's natural command of language. Correct use of language and understanding of the concepts that have been developed prepare children for the formal study of grammar. One of the greatest advantages of Structural Reading is that subject matter that is often considered dull and distasteful by older children is made interesting and amusing to children in grades one and two and makes the later introduction of grammar challenging and welcome.

BIBLIOGRAPHICAL NOTE

1. JEROME S. BRUNER, *The Process of Education* (New York: Vintage Books, 1963), p. 59.

From the Skill of Reading to the Related Reading Skills

In the preceding chapters we have demonstrated how Structural Reading teaches the skill of reading. Once children have learned to read fluently, comprehendingly, and accurately, when they know how to attack unfamiliar words and when they possess a considerable reading vocabulary, they have a foundation on which further progress can be confidently built. First, a child must learn to read, but this skill is not an end in itself. Reading is a means to new goals.

When a pianist has reached the point in his training where his eyes glance over the notes and his fingers simultaneously find the keys on the piano, he is not yet a finished performer. He has the necessary groundwork, but he has much more to learn before he can achieve a correct interpretation of as complex a work as a Beethoven Sonata and can play it with competence and feeling.

The same need for mastery exists in the art of reading. If a child can read accurately and fluently, the groundwork is laid, but he must learn a great deal more before he can read and comprehend as complex a work as Shakespeare. "The good reader," says Dolores Durkin, "is also one who knows the purpose for which he is reading, who adjusts his rate of reading to suit this purpose, who evaluates what he reads, who ponders over what he has read, who is able to laugh with one author, analyze with another, and lose himself in phantasy with still another." [1] This statement throws light on all facets of reading and expresses the goal of all comprehensive reading instruction. Many a child who has learned to read fluently will naturally lose himself in any book that captivates his interest. However, all children need help in reading for more than mere enjoyment; they must learn to read with a detached and critical attitude. Only when these skills are learned will the children be equipped to deal intelligently with subject matter that requires close examination. These abilities are called "related reading skills" or "study skills" in reading. They have been defined by Nila Banton Smith as "skills that are used especially when we want to apply the content read." The child ". . . is using study skills when he reads in science and social studies for the purpose of gathering facts to use in class discussion, in experimentation, in demonstration, in making a report, a summary, an evaluation." [2]

The child can only penetrate into the various school subjects or profit from articles in the field of his special interests if he brings to the text the ability to extract the main idea from a passage, to notice important details, to follow directions, to be able to answer questions that the book or the teacher may ask.

Although Structural Reading has its own new approach to the teaching of reading, it follows modern trends closely in the teaching of the related reading skills. We agree wholeheartedly with Arthur I. Gates, when he says, "The school must set up as one of its objectives the development of more rapid, more varied, and more subtle reading skills than were considered necessary a generation ago." [3]

Our experiences in this field came from work with children, between the ages of seven and twelve, who came to us for remedial tutoring. By analyzing their performances on the Gates Basic Reading Test [4] and the Iowa Tests of Basic Skills [5] we discovered two things: (1) these children needed a thorough foundation in the mechanics of reading, and (2) they should have received a sound preparation for the development of the related reading skills much earlier in their reading instruction.

Our remedial students, without exception, did not read accurately but guessed at words; this vagueness greatly hindered their comprehension of any subject matter. Nila B. Smith illustrates the serious effect of this incapacity in her description of an experiment in a third-grade science book: "The pupil must recognize the pronunciation and the meaning of every word. If he should confuse *steam* and *stream,* for example, this error alone would throw out the experiment." [6] This was exactly the kind of error that we found again and again in working with children who came to us for remedial work.

However, even children who do learn to read well by the sight method must unlearn guessing when they move on to complex subject matter. But no mode of attack that must be unlearned at a later time should ever be taught; a consistent method always builds on what has been learned. In the Structural Reading course children never guess. During the course they are taught to discriminate between words that differ in one or two letters only. They are never permitted, let alone encouraged, to guess what a word says; from the outset they are prepared for the kind of precise reading that will be demanded from them by a science or social study text, where each word may be of crucial importance.

After working with scores of remedial students we came to the conclusion that the development of most of the advanced reading skills should be started at the earliest possible moment, that is, at the beginning of the basic reading instruction and not at its completion. Consequently, in designing the pages for the worktexts in Structural Reading we devised tasks that would develop the needed study skills, but used the simple vocabulary at the beginner's command. We incorporated the following skills from those listed by Gates: [7] 1. Reading to appreciate the general significance of a selection, 2. Reading to understand precise directions, 3. Reading to note details.

A further skill, reading to predict the outcome of given events, was not included in our worktexts for the first and second grades, since it is better suited to more complex reading material in the third grade.

As soon as children can read sentences comprehendingly, the first skill to be developed is the *skill to follow printed directions.* On page 49 of Book B there is a task requiring that the child follow such directions. There are pictures of boys and girls, each with a name written underneath. The text asks the reader to give certain items to each figure; a picture next to each sentence shows what object is to be put into each picture. The instructions are:

> *Give Sam a bat.*
> *Give Ann a hat.*
> *Give Jan a rag.*
> *Give Dick a bag.*
> *Give Jack a fish.*
> *Give Jill a dish.*

The emphasis is on the task of carrying out the instructions. If a pupil is unable to draw the required object, he may draw a line from a pictured item to the figure who should get it. The same kind of task, with harder reading material, is given at the end of Book B.

Page 52 of Book C shows a scene at a beach, with empty squares placed next to some of the pictured objects. The printed directions are now more complicated:

> *Put 1 next to the crab in the trap.*
> *Put 2 next to the clam shell.*
> *Put 3 next to the fish in the net.*
> *Put 4 next to the gull.*
> *Put 5 next to the pit in the sand.*
> *Put 6 next to the lunch box.*

As the reading material becomes more complex, the tasks are made harder. Here are two examples from page 102 of Book D, the second grade worktext.

> *Sam is standing on a ladder.*
> *Steve is raking the leaves.*
> *Give Sam a hammer.*
>
> *Ellen is picking peaches.*
> *Jane is standing next to the tree to help her.*
> *Put a peach in Jane's hand.*

Here the names are no longer written below the figures. The pupil must identify each figure from reading what each one is doing; then he must carry out the directions. This is a much more sophisticated task. The pupil can only give Sam a hammer

PLATE 6

can   cane

pan   pane

van   vane

man   mane

cap   cape

PLATE 7

mend   mend ing

bend   send   call

bend ing   send ing   call ing

PLATE 8

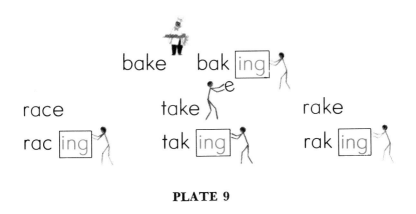

bake   bak ing

race   take   rake

rac ing   tak ing   rak ing

PLATE 9

hop   hopp ing

chop   hit   step   rob

chopp ing   hitt ing   stepp ing   robb ing

PLATE 10

Mix-Ups

The goat is on the coat rack.

The soap is in the stove.

The coat is in the coal bin.

The roast is grazing.

The coal is in the bathtub.

Fix-Ups

The _____ is on the coat rack.

The _____ is in the stove.

The _____ is in the coal bin.

The _____ is grazing.

The _____ is in the bathtub.

PLATE 11

and Jane a peach after he has figured out who is who from the descriptions. He finds the information he needs in the text. In the Iowa Test the following two skills are tested separately: (1) recognition and understanding of important facts and details, and (2) recognition and understanding of *implied* facts and relationships. The above task of following directions teaches children to learn to recognize implied facts.

In other tasks the directions are still more complicated. We have worked out exercises we call treasure hunts, which are great favorites with children. Here the directions are to draw a line from one spot to another, following the clues given at each spot. Sometimes directions are inserted in a story, as on page 120 of Book D (see Fig. 9.1). The text shows how the reading vocabulary has grown.

The hardest task of following directions occurs on page 109 of Book E. (See Fig. 9.2.) Here the pupil reads, "Draw a line over the donkey hitched to a cart." If he does not grasp the exact meaning of the phrase "hitched to a cart," he may make the line above the wrong donkey. The written directions must be read carefully to know which of two similar animals or objects is meant. Only then can each picture be marked correctly. As the comments below show, the reading of the text demands that the child slow his usual pace, since every word has to be taken into account.

As Kathy (7;3) * read each sentence and marked each object, one by one, she commented: "If I had to read it all at once and remember everything, I would have trouble. This way, it is an easy page."

A special case of following directions is involved in another reading skill, namely *map reading.* Map reading helps the adult orient himself; he can find his way in unknown surroundings if he has a map and knows how to follow it. But understanding a map is difficult for a child, because a map depicts in two dimensions what he experiences in three-dimensional space. A child has to *learn* to understand the two-dimensional picture.

---

* Originally we had intended to use Kathy's complete record in Chapter 12 as one of the case studies. However, since she is one of the few children who comment aloud on what they are thinking or doing when carrying out a task, we decided instead to use her records here as an illustration of *how* study skills are developed from task to task.

The Surprise

Farmer Jones went to visit his sick sister.
His farm animals wanted to surprise him.
They did all the work.

The old hen got a big pail
full of water.
Then she scrubbed the barn clean.

Draw a line from the hen to the pail.

The horse grabbed the pitch fork.
He pitched the hay onto a truck.

Make an x on the hay in the truck.

The pig hung the clothes
on the line. The clean clothes
were in a basket.

Draw a line under the basket.

The dog fixed the roof of the barn.
He got up on a ladder with a hammer.
Put a line under the ladder.

Fig. 9.1

The first such task is comparatively easy. The text gives the information that Jack lives next to the drug store. The child has to find the drug store on the map and determine what street it is located on. Figure 9.3 shows not only the original work-text page (page 36 of Book D) but the answers given by one of our pupils, whose comments follow:

Ann (6;7) read: "Jack lives next to the drug store. On what street does he live?" She found the drug store on the map and said as she wrote: "He lives on West Street." She found the answers to the next questions in a similar manner. When she came to the last question, she said: "Oh, that is cinchy. Big Pond. This is different."

Ann was not only able to read the text with full understanding and to orient herself on the map, but she even realized that the last question reversed the previous procedure. All the first

Draw a line over the donkey hitched to a cart.
Put an x under the monkey that is hanging by his tail.
Draw a line around the turkey eating grain.
Draw a line under the donkey drinking water.
Put an x over the purse with money in it.
Draw a line around the money.
Put an x over the monkey who is on the swing.
Put a line over the turkey who is just standing.

Fig. 9.2

questions named a store, and she had to find the street on which it was located. The last question gives the name of the street and asks for a landmark (Big Pond) in that vicinity.

There are many tasks in the worktexts that require map reading; as the vocabulary expands and the facility in reading maps deepens they grow more difficult. The student learns to sketch a route on a map from a description in the text. From such experiences he will become familiar with maps and will learn how to look for landmarks.

The study skills are referred to as *related* reading skills, since the development of one skill leads to the better understanding

Jack lives next to the drug store.
On what street does he live?
Jack lives on *West Street.*

Mr. Smith lives on the same block
where the pet store is.
On what street does Mr. Smith live?
Mr. Smith lives on *Three Tree Lane.*

Jan and Jill live next to the Bike Shop.
On what street do they live?
They live on *Ash Street.*

Pam lives on Hill Street.
She lives next to *Big Pond.*

Fig. 9.3

of another. Children could not follow directions if they had not
learned to note details. There are, however, special pages devoted
to the development of *the skill of noting details.*

In Structural Reading children are asked to find details in
pictures before they are given tasks that require finding details
in a text. After the very first sentences are read the children
must study pictures, find which person in each picture has a
pack, a cap, or a fan, and then write the correct name below

each figure. (See Plate 2.) The same close scrutiny is needed, on page 47 of Book B, to find the names of children who have hidden a bat, a fan, or a dish rag. Later, on page 68 of Book B (see Fig. 9.4), questions are asked for which the pictures as well as the text provide the answers. Some children will use the pictures, others will check the text to find who was on top of

The rat is on top of the cat.

The cat is on top of the dog.

The dog is on top of the fox.

The fox is on top of the ox.

The ox is on top of the box.

Who was on top of the dog?

The _cat_

Who was on top of the fox?

The _dog_

Fig. 9.4

the dog or the fox. Here, for the first time, we have observed that some children reread the text to find the needed information.

The next important step is taken when the answers are to be found in the text only. The pictures now merely illustrate the story. The ultimate goal in developing the skill of reading for detail, of course, is to teach children to learn to *remember* the details of the passage read. It is of immense help to tell children beforehand that after having read a story they should be ready to retell it in their own words, or to answer questions about it. If a child expects such questions, he reads the text with complete attention, eager not to miss an important point.

As the tasks get harder and harder, not all details can be remembered; now the children are encouraged to reread the part of the story that will give the needed information. As will be clear from the following records, children themselves realize that it is sometimes safer to check a text to make sure of a given detail before answering a question. The first record describes a child who was studying the following selection (page 75 of Book D).

YOU'RE ALL WET

It was a cold, wet day. Mother said, "You will have to play in the house today, boys. Don't go out in the rain. And don't play ball inside. You broke my vase last time!" Jim and Bill began to play hide and seek.

Why did the boys have to play inside? because it was raining

Jim was IT. Billy hid in the bathtub. Jim hunted all over the house. At last he said, "I think Billy went outside after all."

Where was Billy hiding? in the bathtub

While Billy was hiding in the tub, Billy bumped into something. The water started to run. He got out of the tub fast.

When Jim saw Billy, he said, "Billy, you are dripping wet! Mother said not to go out in the rain!"

Did anyone go out in the rain? No.

Ann (6;9) was able not only to write the answers to the above selection but also to give a detailed summary of the selection, occasionally checking the text. "It was a cold day and it was raining too. There were two boys, Jim and Billy. Their mother said not to play ball inside because the last time they broke a vase. So they started hide-and-go-seek. Billy hid in the bathtub. Jim couldn't find him. 'Where was Billy hiding?' Bill bumped into a faucet that turns the water on. The water started to run. He got out of the water fast. When Jim saw Billy, Jim said: "You are dripping wet, Billy; Mother said not to get wet."

On further questioning Ann reread the last paragraph and said: "Jim thought Billy had disobeyed the mother and gone out in the rain. But he hid in the bathtub where he got wet."

The tasks consistently increase in complexity. In Book E the child is expected to read longer stories and remember more significant details than he is in the previous books. Questions are asked at the end of a story, and the children are encouraged to reread the text if they are not sure of an answer. Here is a typical task (page 27 of Book E):

WHAT DID JACK FORGET?

"Jack, how would you like to go on a fishing trip with me this weekend?" asked Jack's father.

"Great," said Jack. "Where will we go?"

"To Great North Bay," said Dad. "But while I am at work, you must pack what we need. Do not forget anything. We will need: 2 sleeping bags, the fishing rods, cans of food to last for 6 meals. Then pack raincoats, boots, pants, and socks."

Jack got to work right away. He piled the sleeping bags and the fishing rods in the hall. He dumped the raincoats and boots and extra socks and pants in a pack. Just then his friend Tom came and the boys went out to play.

When Jack's father came home he checked everything in the hall. He called Jack in from the yard.

"Jack, you forgot something. If I had not checked your packing job, we would have been very hungry on the trip. Go check again."

Jack did forget something. He forgot food to last for six meals *Where were they going?* Great North Bay *Who came over to play with Jack?* Tom

Kathy (7;2) doing the above exercise, commented: "Oh, another *What Did I Forget* Page!" She read the page carefully and then said: "He forgot food to last for six days. I remembered that, but I looked back to make sure."

She wrote the answer to the second question, and I asked if she had to look back to answer the second question.

Kathy: "About half and half. I remembered something about Great Bay so I had to look for North."

When she had answered the third question I asked if she had to check back this time.

Kathy: "No, I remembered Tom."

Most of the tasks in the second-grade worktexts contain so many details that even children with good memories cannot answer offhand the questions at the end. This has been done intentionally so that all children will get practice in rereading a text and skimming over a page to spot the details needed for answering a question. Children should be taught that, when they cannot remember any detail, they can remember whether the detail required was given in the beginning, middle, or end of the text, and thus can locate it quickly.

On pages 74 and 75 of Book E there is a two-page story about a mother dog and her seven puppies. Two puppies escape from the basket and Jeff is awakened by their squealing. He finds the lost ones, puts them back in the basket, and goes back to bed. The questions given at the end of the story as well as the answers given by seven-year-old Kathy are listed below:

    1. What is the name of the mother dog? Lady

    2. Which puppy was under the sink? Whitey

    3. Which puppy was under the stove? Frisky

    4. Did Jeff put Whitey back sadly or gently?
    He put Whitey back gently.

    5. Did Jeff go back to bed slowly or quickly?
    Jeff went back to bed quickly.

While Kathy was doing this page she was asked, each time she answered a question, to tell how she arrived at the answer and where she looked for information. Below is the record showing that Kathy tried to answer the questions from memory, but for the most part she checked the text, even when she was sure, knowing each time where the answer was to be found.

First Question: Kathy remembered the name of the mother dog but had to check the spelling. To check she looked at the very beginning of the story.

Second Question: "I have to look who was under the sink." I: "Where in the story will you look?" Kathy: "Not in the beginning. It was about a quarter through. There it is. It says Whitey."

Third Question: "I have to look it up. It was the second puppy, so I'll look at the second half of the story. There, Frisky."

Fourth Question: "I think *gently*. I'll check." (She looked at the top of the second page where it states how Jeff put back the puppy.)

Fifth Question: "*Quickly.* I'll check. That would be at the end of the story."

The reading skill that is the alpha and omega of all skills is *the skill of reading to appreciate the general significance of a selection.* If the teacher begins to develop this skill when children *read* their first story, the task is often too hard; too much attention will be concentrated on the reading itself, so that children have only a vague impression of the content of the story. In this area, too, the teacher should start on the spoken level. If a story is *told,* the children's undivided attention is focused on the development of the story, and they can answer questions about it. The best way for the teacher to find out whether or not the children have grasped the general content of a story is to ask them to retell the story in their own words.

After a good oral preparation it will not be too hard for a child to transfer the effort and concentration needed for understanding, from listening to reading a story by himself. Here, too, by asking pertinent questions, the teacher can guide children to analyze a selection which, if read without pausing to think, is read for pure enjoyment only. What we want to teach them is to sort out what is important from what is peripheral. The teacher must further help the children not to be distracted by what *they* liked best or found important in the story, but to find out the main idea the author was trying to convey.

The task of *choosing the best title* for a story tests the skill of selecting the main theme. At first, the children are given a choice between three titles of which only one sums up the content whereas the others mention insignificant details. It is fascinating to listen to the children give their reasons for their choices.

Following is an example of this type of task (from page 95 of Book D):

At the zoo, Jack and his dog saw a seal doing tricks. The seal barked when a man tossed him a fish. Then the seal held a ball on his nose.

On the way home, Jack said to his dog, "Chips, you can bark like a seal, but can you hold a ball on your nose?"

Chips wagged his tail, and Jack patted Chips on the head.

"You are still the animal I like best," he said. "You are a real friend."

Choose the best title: Seals Like to Eat Fish, Seals Can Bark, Jack and Chips at the Zoo.

The record of Kathy (7;0) as she was completing the above exercise shows that she was able to verbalize her reasons very clearly:

> "*Seals Like to Eat Fish* would be about one thing but it wouldn't be the main thing. *Seals Can Bark*—that is a different thing; it would be a good title but it wouldn't be about the main thing. *Jack and Chips at the Zoo* is the best because it tells the main thing, and it tells about both of them."

Finally, on later pages, the task is no longer to choose one of three suggested titles but to think up a title without any suggestion; the child must learn to epitomize the content himself.

Developing the skill of making up titles prepares children for the next task, condensing a given text. In the worktexts there are tasks that require the condensation of a passage into a telegram of ten words. Here children experience the added difficulty of omitting unnecessary words and recasting spoken sentences into telegram style. As the following record proves, children become aware of the fact that the language of telegram writing is different from ordinary language. We present a record, which clearly shows two steps: formulating the message in the child's own words and then taking out what seems to be dispensable.

Kathy (7;0) read the following (page 111 of Book D):

> *The family was planning to drive to Grandmother's farm. Just as they were about to set out, Mother said, "Dad, we had better call off the trip. Baby is catching a cold."*
>
> *Ann was so sad that Mother added, "We could let Ann go by herself on the train. There is a train that gets there at ten in the morning. Grandmother could meet the train and take Ann home with her."*
>
> *"We must send a wire," Dad said. "Then we will be sure that Grandmother will meet the train."*
>
> *Help Dad write the wire in ten words or less. Be sure to give just the main facts.*

She wrote a first draft that said:

> *Our baby is sick. Meet the ten o'clock train. Ann is on it.*
>
> *Love, Dad.*

Kathy pondered out loud: "Fifteen words—I have to take five words away. Well, you don't need to say *the* train; you can skip *the* and talk like Indians or babies. You can skip *our* and *is*. You don't have to say: "Ann *is* on it. . . . And you don't have to say *love*. Kathy's new version of the wire is reprinted below:

> *Baby sick. Meet ten o'clock train. Ann on it.*
>
> *Dad*

From following and summing up an author's idea, the pupil must one day progress to writing himself; he must learn to organize his thoughts and to make his salient points stand out. It would be too much to expect a child in the second grade to write an extensive book report. But as a preparation for this task, we present (on page 108 of Book E) an actual book report written by an older pupil at our request and ask second-graders to read the report and to cut out whatever is irrelevant to the main topic of the report:

JEFF'S REPORT

Jeff had to write a report on the first airplane for the school paper. The editor told him that it was a very good report, but it was too long. Help Jeff cut his report. Cross out 4 sentences which do not really belong to this report.

"The first airplane was flown in 1903. It was flown by Orville and Wilbur Wright. The two brothers owned a bike shop.

~~"I took a plane last summer to visit my uncle. Jets are faster. Trains are slower. I like plane rides best.~~

"The first flight was made in a glider with no motor. It lasted only a few minutes, but it was the first flight man had ever made. Later the Wright brothers made an airplane with a motor. It could fly 60 miles an hour. It could stay up in the air an hour."

The following record shows how the above exercise was understood by one child, who handled it with assurance and competence.

Kathy (7;1) talked as she crossed out each sentence: "I took a plane—well it doesn't have anything to do with the history of it. Jets are faster—well, that doesn't say anything how fast the first plane could go or anything. Trains are slower—oh really! First, it doesn't have anything to do with planes or the Wright brothers. It tells what Jeff likes."

When asked what would be a good title for the report, Kathy replied: "A good title would be: *'The First Airplane.'*"

Another task (on page 116 of Book E) serves the same purpose. In each story the sentence that does not fit had to be cut out:

In each story cross out the sentence which does not go with that season.

SPRING

Spring is a happy time of year. Birds are making nests and raising families. Flowers are blooming and trees are budding. The days turn warm and sunny. ~~*The children are eager to return to school after the long summer holiday.*~~ *The nights are getting shorter and the days longer.*

SUMMER

Last summer Dale and Betty took swimming lessons at the pool. On the very same day that Dale made his first dive from the diving board, Betty learned to swim the crawl instead of the dog-paddle. "How I wish Mother could see us!" said Dale. ~~*But Mother was home wrapping Christmas gifts.*~~

WINTER

One morning in December, Cliff looked out of his bedroom window. He saw that the ground was covered with two or three inches of snow. "Hurray!" he shouted. "Now I can use my new sled!" ~~*He hurried and put on his swimming trunks.*~~ *He grabbed his sled and ran out to slide with his friends.*

FALL

It was Glen's job to decorate the basement for the Halloween party. On the way home from school he gathered an arm load of red and gold maple leaves. ~~*He picked all the pretty spring flowers that were blooming in the garden.*~~ *By supper time he had the basement all ready for the party.*

Below we present a record that shows one child's complete understanding of the task:

Willa (7;8) commented as she crossed out a sentence in each paragraph. In the spring story: *The children are eager to return to school after the long summer holiday.* "That sentence doesn't belong here, because you don't have a summer vacation in spring. Summer comes *after* Spring."

In the summer story Willa crossed out *But Mother was home wrapping Christmas gifts.* "But Christmas isn't in the summer, is it!"

In the fall story Willa cut out this sentence: *He picked all the pretty spring flowers that were blooming in the garden.* She said: "He couldn't have picked pretty spring flowers, because it was fall."

In the winter paragraph Willa crossed out this sentence: *He hurried and put on his swimming trunks.* Willa commented: "It couldn't be swimming trunks. You don't wear swimming trunks when it's snowing."

The Structural Reading course is designed to build a broad foundation in the first and second grades for the development of the first study skills. We must leave to the higher grades the learning of critical evaluation and analysis of literature; for this study the child must be older and more mature than are beginning readers. Critical reading does not belong at the beginning of the course of instruction but is its culmination.*

We do, however, wish to start the child on the road to critical evaluation and have therefore devised oral tasks as preparation for this skill. For example, we ask questions such as, "Is the story you have read a true story, a story that might have happened, or a fairy tale?" Our records show that even a relatively young child who is a good reader can perform this task.

Kathy (6;10) was asked to read the "Golden Cave" (pages 28-29 of Book E).

I: Is this a fairy tale?

K: I don't think it is. It could be true. It would not happen in Leonia, but it might have happened some place else.

I: If you were a writer and were starting to write a fairy tale, how would you begin? Who would be in it?

K: "Once upon a time." And witches, princesses and princes, a good fairy, would be in it.

I: What happens in fairy tales that does not happen in real life?

K: In real life there are no witches. In real life the animals do not talk.

I: If you were to write a real story what would it be about?

K: I wrote about my kitten Snowball. What I wrote really happened. She can't talk—she is purring so she is a real animal not out of a fairy tale.

Kathy (6;11):

I: Is *Sleeping Beauty* a real story or a fairy tale?

K: A fairy tale—just like *Peter Pan.*

I: Why is *Peter Pan* a fairy tale?

---

* For an excellent analysis of a program designed to develop "creative reading ability" see David H. Russell, *Children Learn to Read.*[8]

K: People can't fly and Peter Pan can. There is a fairy Tinker Bell in it, and there is no such thing as fairies. And also you can't have a dog for a nurserymaid and the children have one.

[Added after a while] Sometimes people write stories that could be true but are not true. In fairy tales they are always not true.

From the skills developed by the end of grade two * those needed in the higher grades can easily be built up. We have shown how the development of the related reading skills is begun in grade one and carefully widened and deepened. In Structural Reading, not only do we incorporate most of the skills recommended by the modern school of reading instruction,[9] but we begin to develop them as soon as a child can read his first sentences. Thus, in our course, we never teach one separate skill at a time. Reading, writing, spelling, and related reading skills are all taught as parts of an integrated whole.

BIBLIOGRAPHICAL NOTES

1. DOLORES DURKIN, *Phonics and the Teaching of Reading* (New York: Bureau of Publications, Teachers College, Columbia University, 1962), p. 16.

2. NILA BANTON SMITH, "Teaching Study Skills in Reading." *The Elementary School Journal* (December 1959), pp. 158 ff.

3. ARTHUR I. GATES, *Teaching Reading,* Department of Classroom Teachers, American Educational Research Association of the National Education Association, 1953, p. 4.

4. ARTHUR I. GATES, *Gates Basic Reading Test* (New York City: Bureau of Publications, Teachers College, Columbia University, 1958).

---

* For a detailed list of the pages on which reading skills are taught see the index at the end of the Teacher's Editions to the Structural Reading Series worktexts.

5. E. F. LINDQUIST AND A. N. HIERONYMUS, *Iowa Tests of Basic Skills* (Boston: Houghton Mifflin Company, 1955).

6. SMITH, *op. cit.,* p. 160.

7. ARTHUR I. GATES AND CELESTE C. PEARDON, *Gates Reading Practice Exercises in Reading* (New York: Bureau of Publications, Teachers College, Columbia University, 1944). Also, Gates, *The Improvement of Reading, A Program of Diagnostic and Remedial Methods* (New York: The Macmillan Company, 1947).

8. DAVID H. RUSSELL, *Children Learn to Read,* 2nd ed. (Boston: Ginn and Company, 1961).

9. *Cf.* Division of Elementary Schools, Board of Education of the City of New York, *Sequential Levels of Growth in the Elementary School* (New York: Board of Education, February 1963).

PART THREE

ADJUSTING
THE STRUCTURAL READING
PROGRAM TO INDIVIDUALS

Providing for Individual Growth

In the previous chapters we have described a method of teaching reading which is consistent with the structural characteristics of the English language. However, in selecting a method of teaching, not only the structure of the subject matter but the nature of children who will learn it must be considered. Who is *the* child who is to be taught?

In all historical periods, education has taken its cue from contemporary views of the nature of the child. In authoritarian times the child was regarded as a miniature adult; at a very early age, he had to learn to work, because adult life held promise only for those who knew how to work hard. More often than not, adult work was difficult and strenuous, so it was thought that school work should be equally demanding and that a child's feelings about it were not to be considered. He must do his tasks whether he liked them or not. Reading was taught this way. The alphabet method of teaching children to read was dry and ill-contrived, but children were expected to do their duty and, obediently, most of them tried to do so.

John Dewey was a leading spokesman for the liberation of children. He demanded that a child's needs and interests be taken into account in his education, so that he might develop into a happy, socially mature, and responsible human being. Unfortunately, some of Dewey's followers misinterpreted his theories. More and more the child was seen as endowed with creative powers and imagination, more and more his adjustment to the group was emphasized, and more and more the child's interests determined the subject matter.

Accordingly, the alphabet method and old-fashioned phonics were thrown out; the newly discovered sight method was adopted in their stead. The advantages of the sight method sounded incontrovertible; no longer was the painful learning of letters or of the blending process necessary. The teacher shows a child a printed word, tells him what it says, and the child will remember it and go on to read books, easily and well, forever after.

Many educators apparently did not recognize that the procedure of associating the shape of a word with its name is solely a feat of rote memory; it does not engage the child's intellectual powers. Not only did such educators, in effect, reduce the process of learning to mere memorization, but they also seemed to have forgotten that the young child has a mind of his own, an active, curious, investigating mind. Richard Hofstadter describes their view of the child in cogent terms. "It was founded upon a primary regard for the child, and avoided making large claims upon his abilities. It made no hopeful assumptions about the child's pleasure in intellectual activity, at least where such activity was difficult, or about his satisfaction in achievement." [1]

Today, largely because of a new national demand for excellence, the prevailing view of the child has changed again. Without neglecting the child's needs and interests, teachers strive to develop his mental powers. They realize that a child can find genuine satisfaction in intellectual achievement. The Structural Reading method was invented for this child, with the help of the children with whom we have worked and who have demonstrated the truth of this new view to us. We hope that our book has shown that children who learn by discovery enjoy the intellectual challenge and excitement of learning to read.

Under the influence of this new view of the child and the growing belief in his intellectual capacities, some educators have come to the conclusion that children can learn the three R's earlier than is customary. The possibility that five-year-olds may be ready to learn to read is reported by Dolores Durkin. Professor Durkin conducted a longitudinal study of forty-nine children who learned to read at home before entering first grade. Interestingly enough "not all are particularly bright; . . . one third had Binet IQ's of 110 or less." [2] In another article she says that "more than half of the early readers came from families of the blue-collar class." [3] Professor Durkin concludes from her study that the intellectual development of children in kindergarten must not be neglected. "Kindergarten programs will be good programs to the extent that they neither frustrate nor bore five-year-olds." [4]

There have, of course, always been bright children who have taught themselves to read at as early an age as four. Our own experiments with Structural Reading have corroborated Professor Durkin's findings. Our five-year-olds enjoyed the readiness program and, at the Castle School, many started on Book B. We have gathered overwhelming evidence to prove that kindergarten children are eager to learn, provided they do not have to memorize by rote but can learn by insight.

But a word of caution seems necessary. Recently attempts have been made to devise methods of teaching very young children to read, children as young as two years old. The reports indicate that these young children have been taught by the sight method, by memorization without understanding. The three-year-olds who learned to read with the aid of electric typewriters learned on a trial-and-error basis; they did not have any insight into what they were doing.[5] Similarly, the Doman approach [6] is based on rote memorization of whole words. A child who learns TOES in big letters by constant exposure to the word is not equipped to read words that have a similar structure (goes, foes). Both approaches utilize the method by which seals are trained to balance balls on their noses and let them drop at a given signal, which is not an approach that develops thinking. If one degrades the teaching of reading to a feat of rote memorization, children are denied the prerogatives of the human race—to think, to discover, to learn by using the mind.

The most important question about reading instruction is *how* it is to be taught. A productive approach to the teaching of reading is effective not only with children of different age groups but with the slow as well as the gifted child. As Jerome S. Bruner says: "Good teaching that emphasizes the structure of a subject is probably even more valuable for the less able student than for the gifted one, for it is the former rather than the latter who is most easily thrown off the track by poor teaching." [7]

A teacher expects her class to include children of a wide range of ability, but she must also know how to cope with differences in readiness to learn and in attitudes toward school, which result from the physical, emotional, and mental make-up of each child, from the socio-economic background of his home, and from the ease or difficulty with which each child adjusts himself to the group. It is one of the advantages of Structural Reading that it can be and has been effectively used with a great variety of pupils.

Providing for individual differences does not require any change in the basic techniques of Structural Reading. It is our firm belief that the established sequence of the method, from sounding out words to sight reading, has equal validity with all children and does not require modification to suit individual differences among students. The adaptation of the program to the individual must be made by shifts of emphasis and of pace, not by changing the method.

Many children will need extra practice to master a particular stage of the learning process. We always avoid teaching any lesson twice in the same way, since it dulls rather than sharpens the children's mental powers. To provide additional help where it is needed, we have devised games for each of the learning stages, which will be described in the next chapter. A child plays these games without becoming aware that they have any purpose other than to give him a good time, yet they provide the practice needed to consolidate his learning. Instead of being numbed by drill on flashcards, children are given games to enjoy which, in the end, result in their mastery of each teaching step.*

The Structural Reading Series worktexts are designed to be used as diagnostic tools with which a teacher who follows the Structural Reading method can determine what difficulties each child is having. Children who have a specific difficulty will need *more* games in order to master a newly learned group of words or the more difficult process of learning to read sentences.

The organization of the classroom situation is, of course, de-

---

* The idea of using games as pedagogical aids is age-old. They have been used by Friedrich Froebel, Maria Montessori, Ovide Decroly and in this country notably by Edward L. Dolch.[8] The games used in Structural Reading were invented by us in teaching the children at the Castle School (1944-1951).

termined by the individual teacher and the school, but there is a growing sentiment in favor of grouping according to ability. As L. Joseph Stone has pointed out: "A teacher . . . must be given plenty of scope for imagination and ingenuity, so that she can fit her teaching to the particular children she is working with. This means that she must have reasonably small groups to work with, so that she can know her children individually and take time to help each over his rough spots." [9]

We have found in actual teaching situations that grouping by ability enables the teacher to help each pupil work at full capacity. All children, slow, average, and gifted, enjoy learning by insight and discovery. But the last group will move faster and will need tasks of a more thought-provoking nature than the others. The first two groups will take more time and will need additional games to help them over their difficulties.

The teaching of writing along with reading in the Structural Reading method makes it easy for a teacher to handle her class by dividing them into ability groups. She can discuss with one group a page in the worktext, and then assign the written tasks to be done independently. This gives the group she is not working with at that moment a constructive task, rather than busy work; at the same time it provides the teacher with a written record of each child's progress.

In culturally deprived areas the teacher faces a special task. Her primary job is to enlarge the children's experiential background and with this their speaking vocabulary. Since the spoken word is the starting point of our method, it must be full of meaning for these children.

On each page of the Readiness Book there are scores of pictures, each of which can be made the starting point for a lively discussion. If the objects pictured are unknown to her pupils, the teacher must spend a great deal of time making the objects themselves, not merely the words, familiar. Children must know what a *map* or a *fan* is, so that when they come to reading these words, they will know what they signify.

The foregoing is especially important for children with a foreign-language background. These children need a great deal of practice with games on the oral level. They must learn to identify new objects, to become familiar with them, and, at the same time, to enlarge their speaking vocabulary. The teacher should use the Readiness Book to encourage all the children in her class to express themselves in adequate and correct sentences. There are scenes in the book intended to stimulate story-telling and the relating of experiences the children may have had themselves.

In every classroom there will be children who find it hard to learn auditory discrimination. Most of them do not pronounce words correctly. Some have actual speech defects, and for these children early speech therapy is advisable. Children with deficient auditory discrimination must be given extra games on the oral level before starting on the Readiness Book. These games give the teacher the opportunity to develop correct pronunciation in a pleasurable situation, without fatigue.

The next step is to help children learn to identify the initial sounds of familiar words. Words with sharply contrasting initial sounds should be introduced first. Once the sounds are heard and distinguished the first major goal is achieved. Special help will be needed again at the next level, when the spoken word is analyzed into its parts. Close scrutiny is needed to hear whether the teacher is saying *mat* or *map, cap* or *cat, bag* or *bat*. By beginning with words that have the greatest possible discrepancies of sound (*bag* and *jam*), the teacher can lead the most ill-prepared children to success. Donald D. Durell,[10] as well as other educators, has emphasized the importance of this vital step in learning to read.

Within any one of the ability groups, there will be some children who have markedly poor visual memories; these are the ones who suffer most under the sight method. The Structural Reading method puts them at no such disadvantage; they can learn to read as well as any other pupils, though they may need a longer time at different levels (see Case Studies 1 and 2, Chapter 12). The hardest task for these children is to master the correspondence of letter and sound. Since these children find it difficult to remember the forms of letters, the key pictures in the Readiness Book are of particular help to them. The teacher does not have to tell them repeatedly what each letter says, or, conversely, by which letter a given sound is recorded; rather, these children can use the key pictures as a dictionary and so become independent of the teacher. They will find a *b* imbedded in the picture of the *b*oot and can hear the [b] when they recognize the object. Their active search and independent discovery of a sound or a letter make the task interesting, and each such exploration will help to establish the sound-letter correspondence. Many games serve to test whether a child is continuing to mix up some letters, like *b* and *d,* or whether he now instantly identifies all letters, so that it is safe to allow him to go on to Book B. The great majority of children have no difficulty in learning to read, once they are ready to begin Book B. The few who still have some trouble are helped by the picture dictionary described in the next chapter. Looking up words on their own, instead of being told what the word says, makes them feel confident and conscious of making progress.

As might be expected, children with poor visual memories very often learn to sound out words readily enough, but find it hard to progress from sounding out to instant recognition of known words (see The Case of Ann, Chapter 12). To overcome this difficulty, we have developed a great many games that provide the practice needed without tedious repetition. While the children are pleasurably absorbed in these games they learn to read words faster and faster until they can recognize them at sight.

Then there are children who have difficulties with spatial orientation. Samuel T. Orton [11] has analyzed these difficulties thoroughly; he advocated kinesthetic exercises to help these children to learn to read. Case Study 3 in Chapter 12 demonstrates how we have helped such a child.

Fortunately, a teacher does not have only pupils who need special attention because one or another step is hard for them. She will also have gifted children who are eager to do more than the work given in the worktext. Until recently the paramount goal in education has been to help slow children keep up with the class, and most classroom teaching has been geared to the tempo and ability of the average child. As Jerome S. Bruner has pointed out: "The top quarter of public school students, from which we must draw intellectual leadership in the next generation, is perhaps the group most neglected by our schools in the recent past." [12]

It is only partly true that bright children learn with or in spite of any method; there are a great many bright children who become bored with school work that fails to challenge their minds. We have found it a joy to teach bright children with our method, for they forge ahead with great enthusiasm and require a minimum of teaching, learning on their own from the work-text pages. Because each new step makes sense, children in this group show the greatest amount of transfer of learning. At each level they need additional activities of a creative, stimulating kind to let them advance at a rate suitable to their native ability. When they study sounds and letters in the Readiness Book, they will make their own sound books sooner than other groups. While working on Book B, they should play more writing games than the others; for example, they can write their own captions for their pictures. They will use the little supplementary book-lets faster and will complete worktexts B and C sooner than the rest of the class. Not only should this group be allowed to read books as soon as they have finished the first-grade worktexts, but the teacher must supply these children with the books they need. Although they will start with beginner books of all kinds, they will soon progress to harder ones. These children especially en-joy starting their own dictionaries. The teacher should write new words on index cards (using different colors for consonants and vowels to facilitate sounding out), and children can file them away in their own index boxes.

The class library should contain a great variety of books, so that no child is condemned to read *below* his ability because the proper books are not available. Since bright children read well very quickly, each one should be given the maximum nourish-ment in the field of his interest. Books that are usually used in second- and third-grade libraries should be moved down to the first-grade library when they are needed.

Just as there are differences among children, there are differ-ences among teachers. A beginning teacher should feel safe with this method, since it outlines a step-by-step course of teaching which will carry her and the class along. Teachers who have been burdened with large classes, with all their individual differences and problems, and who have regretted that many of their pupils have not been able to learn to read and spell, will enjoy the success this method brings to her as well as to her pupils.

In the hands of the teacher who can perform miracles with almost any method of teaching, the Structural Reading method will blossom, since it allows a creative teacher to add original ideas, stories, and games as she goes along. We know that under the leadership of such teachers the method will naturally develop into a rich language arts program which the whole class can master.

BIBLIOGRAPHICAL NOTES

1. RICHARD HOFSTADTER, *Anti-intellectualism in American Life* (New York: Alfred A. Knopf, 1963), p. 356.

2. DOLORES DURKIN, "Reading Instruction and the Five-Year-Old Child," *International Reading Association Conference Proceedings,* Vol. VII, 1962, p. 24.

3. DOLORES DURKIN, "Children Who Learned to Read at Home," *The Elementary School Journal* (October 1961), p. 16.

4. DOLORES DURKIN, "Reading Instruction and the Five-Year-Old Child," *International Reading Association Conference Proceedings,* Vol. VII, 1962, p. 25.

5. NAYA PINES, "How Three-Year-Olds Teach Themselves to Read —and Love It," *Harper's Magazine* (May 1963), p. 58.

6. GLENN DOMAN, *How To Teach Your Baby To Read* (New York: Random House, 1964).

7. JEROME S. BRUNER, *The Process of Education* (New York: Vintage Books, 1963), p. 9.

8. EDWARD L. DOLCH, *Teaching Primary Reading,* 3rd ed. (Champaign, Ill.: Garrard Press, 1960). Also, Dolch, *The Psychology and the Teaching of Reading* (Champaign, Ill.: Garrard Press, 1951).

9. L. JOSEPH STONE AND JOSEPH CHURCH, *Childhood and Adolescence, A Psychology of the Growing Person* (New York: Random House, 1957), p. 257.

10. DONALD D. DURELL, *Improving Reading Instruction* (New York: World Book Company, 1956).

11. SAMUEL T. ORTON, *Reading, Writing and Spelling* (New York: W. W. Norton and Company, 1937).

12. BRUNER, *op. cit.,* p. 40.

Games and Other Teaching Aids

Some of the games described in this chapter are to be used in small groups; others, marked with a double asterisk, can be played by an entire class.

Picture Dictionaries and Functional Games for the Readiness Level

PICTURE DICTIONARIES

On the readiness level some children find it difficult to remember which letter stands for which sound. When in doubt, a child may become upset and these feelings of insecurity undermine his ability to learn. If, at such a moment, the teacher gives him the answer he cannot find himself, the child may be grateful for the answer, but probably will not remember it. If, instead, the child has at hand a means of identifying the corresponding letter and sound himself, he will feel encouraged and his learning ability will benefit. A readiness picture dictionary, such as that which constitutes the first three pages of the Singer *Picture Dictionary*, will give him the means to find his own answers. This dictionary provides the child with the key pictures (see Fig. 11.1 for pictures on page 1) for all the letters of the alphabet. A set of large Key Pictures, hung on the classroom wall in place of the customary

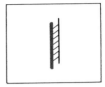

Fig. 11.1

alphabet chart, should also be used as a readiness picture dictionary.

The *Picture Dictionary* and the key pictures become increasingly useful as a child progresses in the Readiness Book. These materials are especially helpful to children who have difficulty in differentiating between two letters with similar shapes, such as *b* and *d*. A child will find the letter *b*, for instance, in the picture of a boot, and without help he can then deduce that *b* says [b]. The same picture helps him through the opposite difficulty, that is, when he wants to write the letter for the sound [b] and has forgotten its form. Among all the pictures only *boot* starts with [b]; it is almost impossible, therefore, for the child to make a mistake. The search for the forgotten letter or sound is made in a spirit of self-help; each time a child looks up a letter he finds it more quickly, and in time he can dispense with this aid. He will now be sure of the correspondence of each letter with each sound.

G A M E S

Games that give practice in discerning initial sounds and learning the correspondence of sound and letter should be played as often as possible in the first stage of learning; the games described below parallel each teaching step.

The first three games listed are devoted to language development, that is, to the expansion of spoken and comprehended vocabulary and to the improvement of diction and pronunciation. It is very important that children learn to express themselves in clear sentences and pronounce words correctly. They should also be able to define the words they use simply but succinctly. The rest of the games provide practice in learning the correspondence between sounds and letters.

**1 / Riddle Games with Pictures. Several pictures are displayed on the board, and each child gets a turn to point to a picture identified by the teacher, who may say "Show me the animal which often purrs and says meow," or "Show me the animal who watches the house and barks when a stranger comes near it." As other pictures are displayed, the teacher may give each of her pupils a turn to describe a selected picture.

2 / Riddle Game Using a Picture Lotto Set. Riddle games can be played with an ordinary picture lotto set. Instead of calling a picture by its name, the teacher describes it. "This card shows an animal that is ferocious and roars. You find him in the zoo." Each pupil should have a turn at playing the teacher's role, as soon as he is able to make up appropriate riddles.

**3 / Game Using Pictures in Books. The teacher opens a picture book to a certain page, looks at a picture, and describes it. "On this page I see a boy with a green apron working with hammer and nails." She then closes the book and gives it to a child who must then find the right picture. The teacher should choose the picture carefully, so that there is only one that fits her description exactly. That is, there may be many pictures of a boy in a green apron, but only one in which he works with hammer and nails. The child therefore must go carefully through the book to find the right picture. Soon a pupil can take over the teacher's role and select and describe a picture which a classmate must then find.

**4 / Matching Pictures and Sounds. The equipment consists of all the key pictures the children have studied to date, and Sound-Picture Cards which show pictures of objects whose initial sounds correspond to the key pictures.

The teacher calls about six children to the front of the class, handing each a key picture which the child will hold toward the class. The cards with the other pictures are placed in a pile on her desk. A child comes up, draws a card from the pile, says *mitten,* and takes it over to the child who holds the *m.* The class will judge if the picture matches the sound. The teacher continues calling on children to draw picture cards and match them with their proper key pictures.

**5 / *What Did I Take Away?* As equipment the teacher should select five or six toys, such as a *b*all, a *j*umping rope, a *c*up, a *p*itcher, and a *d*oll, each of which starts with whatever sounds have just been studied. The teacher places these objects on a tray, which she holds up so that all the children can see the objects. She then asks the children to close their eyes; she picks one object from the tray, hides it behind her back, and tells the children to open their eyes. They must figure out what object is missing, raising their hands when they know which it is. They are not to give its name but its initial sound only, and must define its use or describe its appearance. For example, an answer might be, "You hid something which starts with [c] and you drink from it" (a cup).

6 / Sound Lotto. The equipment consists of a number of master cards—each of which bears a key picture and five blank spaces—and the Sound-Picture Cards—each of which shows an object whose name begins with one of the sounds of the key pictures. The deck is shuffled and placed face down on the table. The number of children who can play is determined by the number of sounds and letters that have been studied.

Each player is dealt a master card. A caller (the teacher in the beginning, a pupil later) draws a picture card and names the object portrayed on it. Each child must listen carefully, identify the initial sound, and whenever his key picture begins with the same sound, he must claim the card. For example, when the caller turns up *fence,* the child with the master card for [f] claims the fence picture and places it on one of the blank spaces on his card. When a child has filled all the blank spaces on his card, he goes out of the game, but the others continue until all the picture cards have been distributed. To vary the game, instead of saying "fence," the caller might describe the object as in the riddle games above.

Sound Lotto can also be played as solitaire. A child lays out several master cards. He then draws a picture card, names the picture on it, places it on the proper master card. He continues until all the picture cards have been drawn.

7 / Snatching Game with Initial Sounds. This game makes use of matched picture and letter cards. For each picture card there is a card bearing the letter that stands for the initial sound of the pictured object. Picture and letter cards are shuffled together and placed face down in a pile. Players take turns drawing cards. When a letter card, for example, *f*, is drawn,* it is put face up to the right of the pile. When a picture card is drawn, it is put to the left of the pile. If the picture card of a sailboat has been turned up, and a player then picks up the letter card *s*, he claims the sailboat and puts the cards together to form a trick. The player having the most tricks wins the game.

One variation is to deal each child a hand of letter cards. Each player then draws, in turn, one card from the pile of picture cards. When a child can match a picture card to one of his letter cards, he has won a trick. If no match is possible, the picture card must be discarded and placed at the bottom of the pack. When a child has found pictures to match all his letters he goes out of the game, but the other children can continue until all the cards are matched. As a variation, the roles of letter and picture cards could be reversed; hands of pictures can be dealt and letter cards can be drawn from a center pile.

8 / Writing Game. Each child gets a pack of picture cards dealt at random from the Sound-Picture Cards (see page 160), which he then sorts into piles, one for each initial sound of the objects pictured, as for example:

(1)	(2)	(3)
mouse	fence	light
man	fan	lemon

---

* It should be remembered that where letters are printed in italics, e.g. *f*, it refers to the written letter. However, in the Structural Reading method throughout grade one, it must always be called by its sound-name, [f], and never by its alphabet name.

He then writes the corresponding letters on lined paper which has been provided.

**9 / *Where Does the Letter Go?* (Dictating Game). The teacher prepares this game by writing each letter to be practiced on a separate line of a sheet of paper. She might have the page reproduced by some method such as dittoing, since there must be one page for each child.

Children enjoy drawing a tiny key picture next to the letters. The teacher starts the game by saying a word such as *mailman;* the children listen to the initial sound and write its letter on the line next to the *m*. The teacher continues with other words and the players write the initial letters on the appropriate lines.

When the children are familiar with this game they may enjoy the following variation. Before the teacher starts dictating, each child is told to guess which letter will win, that is, which row will be the first to have ten letters written on it. Each child should put the letter he has guessed at the top of his sheet. The game then becomes very exciting, and has been a great favorite with children we have taught.

**10 / *Making a Sound Book.* Each child is given a sheet of paper, blank except for letter guide lines drawn at the bottom. The children begin by writing a designated letter on the guide lines, for instance, *f*. They then draw pictures of objects whose names start with [f], such as feather, fan, and finger. They save this paper and subsequent ones using other sounds; when they have completed the Readiness Book, the teacher can staple each child's papers together to form a Sound Book, which he can take home.

Picture Dictionaries and Functional Games for the Beginning Reading Level

READING PICTURE DICTIONARIES

At the beginning reading level some children may need a picture dictionary which can help them to work independently whenever they are not sure of a word. The second part of the

Singer *Picture Dictionary*, designed to accompany Book B, is made up of the top sections of the Book B teaching pages for each group of words (ă-, ĭ-, ŏ-, ŭ-, and ĕ-words). Below each picture the appropriate word, divided into main part and ending, is printed. Each main part is displayed only once. (See Fig. 11.2 for a diagram of an ă-family page.) The testing pages in Book B do not display pictures above the printed words. Occasionally a child may not be certain how to read the word *ran* because he is

Fig. 11.2

not yet sure what *ra* says. He can look up *ra* in the picture dictionary; when he finds it under the picture of a rat, he concludes that it must say [ra] and thus he can decipher the word *ran*.

As children progress in Book B the picture dictionaries become increasingly useful. A child who finds it hard to switch from the ĭ-words to the ŏ-words can look up new main parts and, with continued practice, become more and more confident of his knowledge of all the main word-parts. As on the readiness level, self-help makes the child feel confident because he can work independently of his teacher; this security cannot be achieved if the teacher gives him the answers. In the classroom it has also been found very helpful to hang cards corresponding to the *Picture Dictionary* on the wall.

GAMES

We have found that word-building games are extremely useful teaching aids at this level, and children like to play them. These games are played with the Singer Dominoes, which bear on their faces either main word-parts (*ma, ca, fa*) or final consonants (*p, t, n*), and picture cards that depict objects representing monosyllabic words (*map, cat, fan*). Described here are several kinds of word-building domino games, to be played with appropriate new words as the children progress in their studies. The children benefit most from these word-building games when dominoes from the different groups of words are mixed together. The ă- and ĭ-dominoes should be used together, then later, the ŏ- and ŭ-words. The games can be played repeatedly with any combination of groups in which children need additional practice.

In addition to the word-building games, some children need writing games (see games 7-11) to help them learn to write down instantly, without help, the words they have studied.

Games 12-16 are designed to help children progress from the careful sounding out of words to the instant recognition of them. Though developed for the beginning reading level, these games are useful for remedial work, even in schools that do not use the Structural Reading course. The second-grade vocabulary should then be adapted to these games.

Games 17 and 18 not only help children to recognize known

words faster, but also develop their ability to recognize words that rhyme.

The games described here use ă-words as an illustration; each of the games is suitable, however, not only for the other short-vowel groups and for mixtures of groups, but also for the long-vowel groups.

1 / Domino and Folder Game. This is a game for two players, and in addition to the domino equipment a manila folder is needed. On each side of the folder three rows of three pictures each should be placed. Each picture will represent an ă-word. One side of the folder is assigned to each player. Dominoes bearing main parts are turned face down at the top of the folder; dominoes bearing the endings are displayed face up along the sides. Each player, in turn, picks up a main-part domino and quickly checks the pictures on his side of the folder to see if he can match this domino. If he turns up *ha* he can place it on his picture of a *ham* or his picture of a *hat*. He then completes the word with a domino from the side, saying *m* or *t*. If he has no picture showing an object that starts with *ha*, he must place the domino back in the pool. His opponent then takes a turn. The player who covers up all his pictures with domino words first wins.

This game can be played with two teams of children, each team being assigned to one side of the folder. Players on each team take turns drawing dominoes and building words on their pictures.

2 / Matching Game with Dominoes and Pictures. One set of dominoes is used. The picture cards are divided between each of two players. Dominoes showing main word-parts are placed face down in the center, and those showing final consonants are displayed face up. The first player turns up a word-part domino, *ma.* If he has the picture of a *man,* he selects an *n,* combines the two dominoes to construct the word *man,* reads the word aloud, and places the dominoes below the right picture. If he has no picture that matches the *ma* domino, he returns the domino to the central pool. It is then his opponent's turn. Whoever finds the dominoes for all of his pictures first wins the game.

A variation of this game allows more children to play. The number of dominoes must be increased to accommodate more players. As before, the picture cards are divided between the players and the word-part dominoes are placed face down in the center of the table; however, the leader of the game keeps all the final-consonant dominoes. When a player can match a main-part domino with one of his pictures, he claims the end-consonant from the leader.

**3 / Word-Building Game. The same game can be adapted to classroom teaching. Instead of the small dominoes for the individual child, cardboard dominoes must be provided. A large index card (5 x 8) is cut; two-thirds of the card is inscribed with the main word part and the small remaining piece bears one of the end consonants. In addition picture cards are needed which correspond to the words the children are to build, such as *cat, ham, map*. The pictures are taped on the blackboard, and the children take turns building the respective word below each picture by joining the two parts: *ca n, ha m, ma p*.

4 / Domino Game. In the preceding games pictures were used to make the children say the spoken word and then build the corresponding written word. In the next game, dominoes only are used and the children may build any words they can. The teacher must check to make sure that each word makes sense and is built correctly.

The main-part dominoes are turned down, the ending dominoes turned up. Each player, in turn, picks up a main-part domino and then looks for an ending that will transform it into a meaningful word. This will not always be possible. The children can keep score by counting the number of words they have built. The player who builds the most words wins.

**5 / Domino Game in the Classroom. To use the domino game above in classroom teaching the teacher should again use the cardboard dominoes. The main word-parts should be taped on the board and the cards with the end-consonants placed in the chalk tray. The children then take turns building any word they think up that can be constructed from these parts.

**6 / *Word Game*. The equipment consists of large index cards on which the teacher has written the words to be reviewed and cardboard dominoes of the main word-parts and the endings. The teacher should tape four word cards on the board, such as *cat, nap, mat,* and *ham*. She calls on children to read these words, then turns the cards over and asks a volunteer to come up and build each word in turn with the domino cards. The pupil must remember what the first word was and build it underneath the first card, continuing to build all four words in their proper sequence. To check, the cards are turned face up again. The game continues with a new set of four words. This is a game which can be played with any group of words that is being studied.

**7 / *Writing Stories*. The writing game our students liked best we call "Writing Stories." In this game, the single words children are able to write down from dictation are used in an interesting story, which is told to them.

The teacher distributes a sheet of ruled paper to each child and explains that she will tell a story and pause to dictate a word which the children should write down. In the following sample, those words that the children can write at this stage in the course are printed in roman:

> *Once upon a time, there was a* cat. *The cat had no home and looked for a place to live. It so happened that there was a* man *who had moved to a new neighborhood; he needed a cat because mice were eating his grain. So, one day he took a* bag *and went out to look for a cat. He got tired from walking and sat down to have a* nap. *When he woke up, he hardly believed his eyes. There was our cat sitting next to him in the grass. He took her home and no mice, nor a* rat *either, ever came near his house again.*

Children like to listen to such stories and are proud to be able to write down the names of the characters and objects that the stories tell about.

8 / *Writing Game with the Stop-and-Go Cube*. This game makes use of an invaluable device, the Stop-and-Go Cube. Any die can be used; two opposing faces should be covered with red tape, the other four with green tape. Each player gets a turn at throwing the die. If a player throws red, he passes on the die to the next player. If he throws green, he must write a word that his opponent selects from Book B and dictates. The players take turns until one of them has managed to write down ten words. He wins and the game ends.

**9 / *The Word Sequence Game*. The teacher writes four or five words on index cards and displays them to her class in a pocket chart. Then she turns the cards over and tells the children to write the words from memory on a piece of paper. Since the words are unconnected, it is hard to remember them in their sequence. Therefore the children should be encouraged to make up a story or, perhaps, a sentence, using the words to help them remember the word order. If the words *pup, tub, sun,* and *run* have been given, children may make up a sentence such as, "Give the *pup* a bath in a *tub,* and let him *run* in the *sun* to dry." This adds zest to the task of writing down a sequence of given words.

**10 / *The Sorting Game*. This game can be played after the ă- and ĭ-words have been studied. The equipment consists of sheets of paper divided into two columns, one labelled with the key word *man*, the other with the key word *bib*.

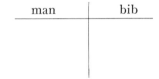

The teacher should give a riddle describing an ă- or an ĭ-word and the children must solve the riddle and write the word in the correct column on their sheets. All ă-words must be written in the column headed by the word *man;* all ĭ-words go under *bib*. For instance, the teacher might say, "I am thinking of an animal that loves the mud and that grunts." The children would guess the word *pig* and would write it in the column under *bib*. The game can be varied by a pupil dictating from among the words in the first two units of Book B. Or the teacher may dictate one word and then ask the pupils to think of a rhyming word, which they must write underneath the first word.

As pupils progress through Book B more columns should be added, so that in the end each pupil knows how to analyze the five short-vowel groups correctly. To supplement the study of Book C similar columns should be drawn, using final and initial consonant blends (*lamp, sift, drop, drum, step*), again grouping the words according to the short vowel. Once the magic *e* is introduced, columns with *lake* and *slide* should be used as well as *pan* and *pane* or *pin* and *pine*.

11 / The Sorting Game with the Stop-and-Go Cube (Two Players). This is a slight variation of the previous game, adapted for two players or a small group, in which, in addition to the sheets of paper mentioned above, the Stop-and-Go Cube, described on page 168, is used.

The first player throws the die. If the red side comes up he loses his turn; if the green side comes up, he may write the word the teacher or another player dictates from the first two units of Book B. All ă-words must be written in the column headed by the word *man;* all ĭ-words go under *bib*. The game continues until one player's sheet is filled with an agreed-upon number of words, twelve or fifteen perhaps.

12 / Word Lotto. Word Lotto is an extremely helpful game. Eighteen large master cards are divided among the players. On each card a vertical line is drawn down the middle; on the left, one of the studied words (*cat, hat, man*) is printed. The right side is blank; it is to be filled with a corresponding picture.

A student acts as caller. He holds a pile of small cards; on one side of each card is a picture and on the reverse, the word that names it. The caller holds up each card in turn with the *word* facing him. He reads *cat* and turns the card to the picture side to check whether or not he was right. The pupil who has the master card with the word *cat* on it claims the picture and places it on the correct blank space. Each player has to scrutinize quickly all the words on his cards to find if he has the word the caller has announced. This develops his ability to read words at a glance. The caller, too, makes progress in reading the words quickly at sight.

This game can be played by one child alone. The child goes through the small cards, reads each word aloud, then checks it by turning over to the picture; he then finds the correct word on the master card. A teacher observing the child will be able to discover which words the child still sounds out in parts, and she should use these words in other games to speed up the child's reading.

This game becomes more interesting and more profitable if words from two or more groups are mixed together.

13 / Snatching Game (Two Players). Eighteen word cards and eighteen matching picture cards are needed. The two sets are shuffled together and placed as a dummy pile between two players. The first player turns up the top card—for example, the picture of a *hat*—and puts it in front of him. The second player turns up the next card. If the card he turns up has the word *hat* written on it, he snatches his partner's card and puts the cards together, making a trick. The game continues until there are no more cards. The player with the most tricks wins.

14 / The Matching Game (Two Players). Word cards and picture cards are kept separate. A pile of word cards is placed face downward in front of one player, a pile of matching picture cards in front of the other. Both players simultaneously turn over their top cards. The first one to see that a word and a picture match calls the word and wins the trick. If the cards do not match, they must be placed at the bottom of the player's pile. The game continues until all of the cards have been matched. The player with the most tricks wins.

15 / The Dummy Game. The word cards are shuffled and put in a dummy pile. An equal number of picture cards are dealt to each player. One dummy card after another is exposed and the players read them *silently*. Each time the child who has the corresponding picture card deposits it in a box in the middle of the table. The player who discards all his cards first wins.

16 / Dominoes and The Stop-and-Go Cube. Putting the dominoes back into their box after a game has been played can be made into a second game, which gives the players practice in reading words at sight. For this variation the stop-and-go cube, described in Game 7, is used. A player throws the die. If it is red he passes it on. If it is green he reads one of his words aloud and places the dominoes forming that word in the box. The players take turns, and whoever gets all his dominoes back in the box first wins.

17 / Yours or Mine? (Two Players). The equipment for this game consists of ten sets of four rhyming word cards, a total of forty cards in all. One word of a set appears at the top of each card, along with an illustration; on the other three cards of the set, a different word from the group appears at the top and is illustrated.

The cards are shuffled and the deck is placed face downward in the middle of the table between two players. The first player picks up a card, reads the four words on it aloud, and places it in front of him. His opponent picks up the next card and reads its four words aloud. If the words belong to the same rhyming set, he can claim his opponent's card and put it with his own. If his opponent then happens to draw the third card that belongs to this rhyming set, he may take both cards and place it on his side. A trick is completed only when a player collects all *four* cards in the rhyming set. Thus the cards may travel back and forth three times before a trick is assembled. The player who takes the most tricks wins.

18 / Slapjack (Two Players). This game uses twenty pairs of rhyming word cards, a total of forty. Each pair consists of two cards on which one word only is printed. The cards are shuffled and distributed equally between two players, so that each player has a pile of cards, face downward, in front of him. Both players turn over a card at the same time and place them next to each other. If the words do not rhyme, the next two cards are turned and placed on top of the first ones. When the words do rhyme, for example, *lock* and *rock,* both players slap their fists on the table. The player who slaps first takes his opponent's pile of discards and adds it to his stock pile of cards. The game ends when one player has no more cards.

In one variation, the pairs of rhyming word cards are separated and shuffled. Each player places his pile of cards face downward in front of him. Both players turn over the top card of their piles simultaneously. The player who first discovers two rhyming cards wins that trick. As cards with words that do not rhyme are turned up they are displayed on the table. If a newly turned card rhymes with any that have been turned up, the player who slaps the table first gets the trick. The game ends when all cards have been formed into tricks. The player who has the most tricks wins.

Games for the More Advanced Reading Level

Here we present games that children in the second grade and above like to play. Games 4-6 have been devised to give pupils practice in building sentences and in reading them fluently and meaningfully. In addition, all the games previously described can be adapted to the new vocabulary taught in the second grade.

1 / Quartet Game. This game uses forty cards, divided into ten rhyming sets of four words, as in Game 18, *Yours or Mine?* on page 172. The words themselves, of course, are more advanced than the ones used in *Yours or Mine?*

Cards are dealt to four or five players. The object of the play is to assemble sets of the rhyming groups. Each player takes a turn asking some other player for a card he needs; if a player holds a card with the top word *cake* he could ask for *rake*. If the player who is asked has the *rake* card he gives it to the first player, who goes on asking until the player he asks does not have the card demanded; it is then that player's turn. The players, of course, have to remember whom they have asked for what cards. When a player assembles a set of four rhyming word cards he has won one trick; whoever collects the most tricks wins.

2 / The Memory Game. This game gives children practice with the most difficult words from Books D and E. It also aids instant word recognition.

The equipment for this game consists of sets of matching cards, one showing a word and the other a corresponding picture. The picture cards are placed face down in a pile. The word cards are scattered in the center of the table, face down.

The first player takes the top card from the picture pile and names the picture, for example, *park*. He then turns up any word card and reads it aloud; if the word matches, the trick is his. If, however, it bears a different word, for instance, *goat,* he must put the picture card *park* at the bottom of the picture pile and leave the card with the word *goat* in the pool, again with the face turned down. He should try to remember where in the pool the card with the word *goat* is located. If in the course of the game he draws the picture card that shows the goat, he must try to turn up the word card for *goat.* Whoever has the greatest number of tricks, when all cards are finally matched, wins.

Some of our pupils liked to make this game harder by scattering both sets of cards face down on the table. Each player turns up a picture card and a word card at the same time. He now must try to remember the position of both the picture and the word card.

3 / Old Maid. This game should be played with whatever words a pupil has read incorrectly. The teacher writes these words on index cards. There are two cards for each word, one bearing the word written in blue and red (blue for the consonants, red for the vowels) and the other bearing the word written in black. In addition, there is one card bearing the word *WITCH* in black letters. The cards are shuffled and dealt one at a time to each player. Before the play begins each player takes out all his matching pairs of cards and puts them down as tricks. Then, in turn, each player offers his remaining cards, fanned out and face down, to his neighbor, who picks one card out. If the card chosen matches a word in the chooser's hand, he has won a trick. The game goes on until one player is left with the *WITCH* card; he is the loser.

4 / Mix-Ups and Fix-Ups. Forty cards are used, on each of which is written half of one of the twenty broken-up sentences. Each sentence is broken into its subject and its predicate, one on each card. Each subject card forms a meaningful sentence only when combined with its own predicate card.

Subject card	Predicate card
The ship	has a mast.
The doll	is in the crib.

Possible sentences include the following (vocabulary from Book C):

1. A hen   has wings.
2. The clock   says tick tock.
3. Mom   mends a sock.
4. The ship   has a mast.
5. The doll   is in the crib.
6. A man   drives the truck.
7. The tree   is full of buds.
8. The dress   hangs on a rack.
9. The bulb   is in the lamp.

All cards are shuffled and placed face down in the chalk shelf. The teacher calls on various children to take turns turning up the top card, reading it aloud, and putting it to the left in the pocket chart if it is a subject card, to the right if it is a predicate card. The children should read the resulting nonsense sentence. If they wish, they can choose such a nonsense sentence and make a humorous illustration for it.

This game can be easily adapted to two players using the same equipment. All cards are shuffled and placed face down on the table between the players. The players take turns turning up the top card, reading it aloud, putting it to the left if it is a subject card, to the right if it is a predicate card. When one card forms a meaningful sentence with another that has already been turned up, the player reads the complete sentence and takes both cards as his trick. The player with the greater number of tricks wins.

Each time, when he takes a card and is looking for the proper complement, the player should be allowed to read a nonsense sentence aloud, such as "a hen drives the truck," "Mom is in the crib," etc.

**5 / A Sentence Game. The equipment consists of thirty word cards using any group of words that will give pupils the practice they need, and thirty sentence cards, each of which bears a sentence, with one underlined word, that word being one which also appears on a word card.

Word cards and sentence cards are shuffled separately. One child is the leader and holds the sentence cards. The word cards are dealt to the children in the class, one to each pupil, who place the cards in front of them. The leader reads the first sentence, slightly emphasizing the underlined word. The child who has the underlined word asks for the sentence card and places it on his word card. To make this game harder, each child could read his word card carefully and place it face down; the children must remember their words in order to claim the sentence card.

This game can be adapted easily to two players or to small groups. Several word cards are dealt to each player, who places the cards face up (at a later stage, face down) in front of him. The leader reads the first sentence, slightly emphasizing the underlined word. The player who has the underlined word asks for the sentence card and places it on his word card. The player who has all his word cards covered first is the winner. Children should take turns being the leader.

6 / Crossing-Out Game. The following game gives practice in spelling. The teacher can use this game to practice any group of words.

The equipment consists of thirty index cards, on each of which the teacher has written one word. The teacher should divide the class into two teams. She dictates half of these words to one team, the other half to the second team. The children write these words down, one below the other, on a sheet of paper. The word cards are then shuffled and placed in a pile, face downward, on the desk. The teacher (or a leader chosen from the children) draws a card and reads it aloud, and the pupils who have this word on their list cross it out. He then places the card at the bottom of the pile. The game goes on until one team has crossed out all their words. This is the winning team.

This game can be easily adapted to two players or to small groups. Again the teacher writes the words on index cards and then dictates these words to the players, who write them down. The word cards are then shuffled and placed in a pile, face downward, between the players. Each player in turn draws a card, reads it, and crosses that word off his list. He then places the card at the bottom of the pile. The game goes on until one player has been able to cross out all his words.

Suggestions for Remedial Work

A special adaptation of the Structural Reading course is necessary for children who need remedial work. Many of these children, having been exposed to sight reading for one or more years, have grown accustomed to guessing instead of reading words. They will need help both to stop guessing and to learn the characteristic structure of words. In most cases it is advisable for the remedial specialist to take her students through all the Structural Reading Series books, from the very beginning, using at the same time the games described thus far. Remedial students who have had some phonic training have often learned more about consonants than about vowels; therefore, they must learn how to discriminate between vowel sounds. It is of the greatest importance to begin with the short vowels and go on in the prescribed Structural Reading sequence. Therefore, the games we have found most helpful in remedial work are the word-building games with the dominoes, the sorting games with the Stop-and-Go Cube and the writing games.

Preliminary Test Results and Four Case Studies

During the past twenty years many children have been taught to read by the Structural Reading method. At the Castle School, from 1944 to 1951, we taught five-year-olds reading, writing, and arithmetic, and subsequently we gave private reading instruction to five-year-olds who were attending public school kindergartens. They started the reading process with us and knew no other method but ours.

The individual records of each of these five-year-olds show that learning to read can be a challenge as well as a pleasure. Their scores on the Gates Primary Reading Tests show that after completing the first-grade books of Structural Reading, they read as well as eight- or nine-year-olds do at the end of the second or the beginning of third grade. In following up these children, we found that without exception they are in the top reading groups at their schools; moreover, they read voraciously on their own because they really enjoy reading.

During the 1963-1964 school year, the Structural Reading program was tried out in twenty-four classrooms including several pilot projects scattered across the country. This book was written before many of the experimental classes had completed Book C, and thus before test results could be obtained for these classes. All the teachers reported that the children enjoy learning to read with this method and that they are reading at a high level of interest. Those classes that were tested after completing Book C confirm these estimates and the available data show a consistent pattern. The experimental classes taught by the Structural Reading method received significantly higher scores on standardized tests than comparable groups do.

After his visits to the experimental classes Dr. Charles M. Shapp, Assistant Superintendent of the schools involved in the New York City pilot project, wrote:

I brought in several beginning readers that the children had never seen. The children swarmed around me for an opportunity to look into these books. The teachers told me that this exuberant interest in reading is a new phenomenon. When the children read to me, it was quite clear that they had made marked progress in attacking new words. Whatever errors they made, few were in initial sounds. The success in attacking the initial sound seems to have given the children a sense of confidence and willingness to try to work out the pronunciation of the full word. The experimenting teachers are unanimous in their certainty that these children had made exceptional progress. Test results objectively verify these findings.

In one school a teacher reports that a group of parents have come in and delightedly asked what the teacher had done to make these children such avid readers at home. I observed this myself during my brief visits. The books that I brought in and from which the children read soon were dispersed to various desks, with two or three children poring over each of them. I virtually had to wrest the books from the children and succeeded in doing so only because I promised to send them a gift of five books for their library.

We are so enthusiastic about the results that we are now laying plans for extending the Structural Reading Program at least to the entire first grade and kindergarten of the three experimental schools.

Emanuel R. Brandes, principal of P.S. 39 in Harlem, commenting on the use of Structural Reading in a first-grade class at his school noted:

Both class and teacher responded enthusiastically to the Structural Reading program. The reading results were phenomenal in comparison with those formerly achieved by other children of like ability in our school. . . .

Sylvia Lentz, the teacher of the original Structural Reading class at P.S. 39, summarized her observations as follows:

. . . Structural Reading is the best reading approach I've yet encountered. The Structural Reading Series provides the child with a variety of

skills, with emphasis on comprehension, development, and word attack. Reading becomes an enjoyable and rewarding experience.

At present, preliminary test results are available for two pilot classes of the Structural Reading program. The first set of scores, obtained from an above-average class, was rated by the school administration as 1-1, a top first grade. They were compared with another 1-1 class from a neighboring school in the same culturally deprived area. The latter was taught with a leading basal reading series supplemented by a phonics program. Both teachers were rated excellent by the school staffs. Both classes were given the New York Tests of Growth in Reading after completing the Grade One programs. The results are listed in Table 1.

By scanning the table it is seen that every child in the experimental group (Structural Readers) tested at grade 2.5 and above, compared to ten of the eighteen in the control group, while eight

TABLE 1

Structural Readers	Median Grade Score	Basal Readers	Median Grade Score
*E1	3.5	*C1	3.4
E2	3.3	C2	3.2
E3	3.3	C3	3.1
E4	3.3	C4	3.1
E5	3.2	C5	3.1
E6	3.1	C6	3.0
E7	3.1	C7	3.0
E8	3.0	C8	3.0
E9	3.0	C9	3.0
E10	3.0	C10	2.9
E11	2.9	C11	2.4
E12	2.9	C12	2.4
E13	2.9	C13	2.3
E14	2.8	C14	2.3
E15	2.8	C15	2.2
E16	2.6	C16	2.2
E17	2.5	C17	2.2
		C18	2.1

*E = Experimental Group; C = Control Group.
The numbers following these letters designate individual students in the groups.

of eighteen children in the control group tested below 2.5. The statistical comparison between the two groups is given in Table 2, and shows that the Structural Reading group scored significantly higher than the control group.

In another pilot class a 1-4 group, which had a mean IQ of 99, was taught with Structural Reading. At the end of the year the class was given the Gates Word Recognition Test and the Sentence Reading Test. The school administration was amazed to find that in the test group, ten of the twenty children scored above the 90th percentile in Word Recognition and eight of

T A B L E   2

	Number	Range	Mean	SD	t value
Experimental	17	2.5-3.5	3.0	.26	2.4*
Control	18	2.1-3.4	2.7	.43	

*Thirty-three degrees of freedom; significant difference at the 96 percent confidence level.

sixteen scored above the 90th percentile in Sentence Reading. Because of the high scores, the school compared the class's achievement with a 1-1 class that showed scores above the 94th percentile in Word Recognition with seven of twenty-six scoring above the 94th percentile in Sentence Reading. It is apparent that these tests, although designed for Grade One and for the first half of Grade Two, are not an adequate measure of the capabilities of either of these groups, since so many scored near the top. The experimental group, for instance, had more scores in the 99th percentile (six of twenty) than in any lower decile range, giving a curve skewed excessively at the top and preventing valid comparisons. The grade scores are perhaps more meaningful and are shown in Table 3, along with the IQ's of both classes. The statistical comparison is shown in Table 4.

It is apparent that the experimental group, which scored fifteen points below the comparison class in IQ and which was rated next to the bottom in this school, advanced through the Structural Reading program, both in Word Recognition and Sentence Reading, to a level matching that of the highest rated class, which was taught by one of the leading basal reading pro-

TABLE 3

Structural Reading Class (1-4)			Compared Class (1-1)		
IQ*	PWR†	PSR‡	IQ*	PWR†	PSR‡
—	3.7	3.2	123	2.6	2.7
113	3.7	3.6	121	2.2	2.8
—	3.6	—	120	2.2	2.7
105	3.6	3.3	105	2.6	2.7
117	3.6	3.2	127	2.6	2.6
105	3.3	3.4	110	2.7	2.7
91	2.8	2.7	122	3.4	3.6
113	2.8	2.7	111	2.4	2.6
83	2.8	—	108	1.7	2.3
83	2.6	2.8	108	2.4	2.8
102	2.5	2.4	100	—	2.6
122	2.4	1.7	140	2.9	3.1
99	2.4	2.7	104	2.4	2.9
99	2.3	2.0	121	2.3	2.2
90	2.0	2.4	120	2.9	3.0
83	1.7	—	137	2.6	3.0
100	1.7	1.4	121	3.2	3.4
90	1.6	—	114	—	2.3
93	1.6	1.6	101	2.2	2.3
—	1.4	—	113	2.3	2.5
			90	1.5	2.1
			106	2.3	2.7
			133	2.6	2.1
			132	2.9	3.2
			104	2.6	3.3
			95	—	2.4

*The IQ's were obtained from the Pintner General Abilities Tests (Verbal Series).
†Gates Word Recognition Test, Grade Score.
‡Gates Sentence Reading Test, Grade Score.

grams supplemented by phonics. Since the difference in IQ is significant between the classes, the gain in reading ability is significant. Obviously additional controlled experiments and research in testing are needed before the final verdict is in. The benefits in these comparisons, however, are quite apparent.

Structural Reading has also proved effective in remedial classroom situations. In one class of severely retarded second graders in the New York City school system the whole group tested at the Readiness level in the Fall but achieved grade two scores by the end of the first year of the Structural Reading program.

T A B L E 4

Intelligence Quotient				
	Number	Range	Mean	SD	t value
Experimental	17	83-122	99	12	3.96*
Comparison	26	90-140	114	12	

Word Recognition Test				
	Number	Range	Mean	SD	t value
Experimental	20	1.4-3.7	2.6	0.78	0.56†
Comparison	23	1.5-3.4	2.5	0.42	

Sentence Reading Test				
	Number	Range	Mean	SD	t value
Experimental	15	1.4-3.6	2.6	0.69	0.65‡
Comparison	16	2.1-3.6	2.7	0.40	

*41 degrees of freedom; significant difference at the 99.9 percent confidence level.
†No significant difference.
‡ No significant difference.

For more than twenty years, we ourselves have taught remedial reading individually to more than a hundred students. These children were in various grades in elementary schools, and they were failing in reading and in allied subjects. With most of these pupils we found that it was the method by which they had been taught, not the children themselves, that had failed. They had not been able to learn to read by the sight method, even when it had been supplemented by phonics. We were able to teach every one of these children to read using Structural Reading, even those who had several years of failure behind them. Although our worktexts were designed for children in the first two grades, the older children profited by them and enjoyed reading them, since they were proud to be able to do the tasks set in the books and also were amused by the absurdities on many of the pages. They learned to read not only the worktexts but also books they had been unwilling to tackle before they started remedial work. It sometimes took a long time to help a child unlearn all the bad habits he had acquired, such as looking at a word not at its beginning but at its middle or end for "clues," using the alphabet names instead of the sounds of letters, and, most dangerous of all, trying to guess instead of to read. But once a sound foundation was laid, progress was noticeable not only to us but to the child himself. It is very gratifying to see a child who has been repeatedly defeated and has come to despair of his ability to learn to read, grow in confidence, show his newly gained skills at school, and cease to be plagued by fear.

Not one pupil taught with this method has failed to learn to read. Among our remedial students there were slow and average children who were brought up to the grade standard and were then able to keep up with their classes without further remedial help. There were also bright children who subsequently performed outstandingly in school. One case study which has previously been published [1] describes an eight-year-old boy, Eric, who could not read a word, although tests showed that he was of above-average intelligence. Eric had suffered deeply not only because he could not learn to read but because he had been taken out of his class, third grade, and put in a group with retarded children. Taking one lesson a week from December 19 to June 23, with follow-up lessons in summer camp, he was able to go back to his old class. He had caught up with the pupils beginning grade four and could easily go ahead with them, having regained confidence and pride in his achievements.

The records of our remedial students point up the shortcomings of the sight method. Their learning is a relearning and does not, therefore, elucidate the nature of learning to read from its very beginning to its successful conclusion. For this reason, we present only one remedial case, and that only to round out the picture of the Structural Reading course.

In the following pages we present three detailed case studies of five-year-olds; their comments reveal the learning process as it takes place in Structural Reading. These research studies should be of interest not only to teachers but to psychologists as well. As Kurt Lewin [2] has pointed out, individual cases, thoroughly studied and analyzed, contribute as much to the understanding of a problem as statistical data.

The case studies we have chosen to present are of children

who learned to read despite some specific difficulty. In each instance our records show how the teaching course was adapted to fit the needs of an individual child.

The Case of Michael

Michael was brought to me * at the age of five and a half. His parents had been told by an ophthalmologist that his vision was so poor that he would have serious trouble learning to read. Michael had only peripheral vision in the right eye (glasses 20/100), so he could not use that eye for reading. He was farsighted in his other eye (glasses 20/30).

Michael's parents asked me to teach Michael privately while he went to a public-school kindergarten. For the first four months Michael had three lessons a week; subsequently he had four lessons a week, sometimes five.

Michael started on September 9th. It became apparent immediately that the greatest hurdle for him would be to learn the letters. It took Michael much longer than it would take most children to learn to distinguish between *m* and *f,* the first two letters in the Readiness Book. They are usually mastered in two lessons. Since it took Michael six lessons to be absolutely sure of these letters, I proceeded very slowly. We repeatedly played games that helped Michael to remember what each *letter says—* Picture Lotto, Snatching Game, and the Folder Game. Whenever Michael picked up a card with a letter and was unsure of it, he looked it up in the picture dictionary; thus he never experienced any sense of failure. At the beginning Michael was a hasty child; even his speech was that of a boy in a hurry. He often mumbled when he pronounced words. Since so many of the games we played required careful pronunciation, his diction improved markedly. Because he enjoyed the games, he lengthened his attention span.

Michael's coordination was very poor, so we played many writing games. Michael's favorite game was using the writing ma-

---

* The records excerpted in the earlier chapters of this book were taken from the files of both authors. The cases in this chapter have been taken from the files of Toni S. Gould.

chine.* Naturally a curious and mechanically-minded child, he liked the writing machine so much that his letters improved markedly; he even began to enjoy writing letters without the machine. We played a writing game with the Stop-and-Go Cube nearly every lesson, and he was intent on filling the pages in his notebook with letters, greatly improving his penmanship.

Below are two of Michael's comments which show his understanding of the lessons.

When Michael was studying the *s* in an early draft of the Readiness Book, he came across a poor picture and said: "Soap? It must be soap; it looks like butter but butter wouldn't work."

Michael peeked ahead in the workbook to see what was coming: "That is a shirt, so the new sound is [sh]. That's what I hear."

We spent an unusually long time—three months—on learning the letters. It is interesting that Michael also took a disproportionately long time in learning the capital form of the letters. We continued practicing them through the end of January.

From the moment Michael mastered all the letters he speeded up his rate of progress tremendously, because from then on he could rely on his intelligence. Throughout the course, he used the picture dictionary to check words of which he was not absolutely sure. With this help, Michael mastered each new step with steadily increasing confidence, as the following excerpts show.

December 12th	*Read*	*Commented*
	meat[?]	The picture isn't so good.
	ha m, ham	It's a ham.

He enjoyed the work with the dominoes and the Folder Game immensely and felt very confident of his ability to build, read, and write words. Michael picked up the *fa* domino and put it on the picture of a fan without any help. "I knew it had to go there. I thought it up in my brain."

The step from sounding out words to reading them at sight was not easy for Michael. Before starting the reading of sentences we played many games to help him achieve the recog-

---

* The writing machine is a simple device which by turning on a light reveals letters to be traced. Information about its eventual availability can be obtained from The L. W. Singer Company, Syracuse, N. Y.

nition of words at sight. Rhyming and sorting games helped him most.

December 13th	Read	Commented
	Ann has a cat.	Ann has a cat! [I showed him the picture.] I already read it.

December 16th. We started on the ĭ-words only three weeks after we began the study of the ă-words.

Read	Commented
fi g, fig	I can't even tell from the picture. I figured it out, it's a fig. You can figure out the word.

January 8th. We started the ŏ-words on the spoken level. He could now read sentences fluently.

Read	Commented
A man ran	to catch the bus.
Dad has a sock.	But he has another sock.
Ann sat on a rock.	And she ran off, because a big wave was coming, because this was near the seashore.

When we played the rhyming game, Michael exclaimed "Box and ox—that makes a trick. I can even feel it rhyming."

Michael went through the rest of Book B very rapidly as the dates show.

January 21st. We started on the short-ŭ words.

January 28th. We started on the short-ĕ words.

February 7th. We started on Book C. Michael again enjoyed the games with the folder. This time, instead of dominoes, I used cards with words matching the pictures in the folder. As he read the first two cards he said: "There are too many easy words with this one. Do you call *ill* hard? And *rock* is a cinch."

Michael progressed through Book C without any difficulty, surprised and pleased that he could read words that he had not seen before.

February 8th	Read	Commented
	pump	I never had the word *pump*—never in my life.

went   I never learned that one before. If I
         haven't learned it, and I can read it—
         that is very good.

February 14th. We started work on words that have an initial consonant blend; at the same time we continued playing the games that lead to the fluent reading of known words.

March 4th	*Wrote*	*Commented*
	brick	I never had this word before. I never even read it.

April 1st	*Read*	*Commented*
	ring	I have never even read this word.
	April	[I had written the date in his notebook.] That says April. I figured that one out by myself.

The study of the magic-*e* words proceeded at great speed because Michael understood the principle.

> *April 5th*. We worked with the long-*a* words
> *April 10th*. We worked with the long-*i* words
> *April 15th*. We worked with the long-*o* words
> *April 18th*. We worked with the long-*u* words
> *April 22nd*. We worked with the long-*e* words

At this point reading instruction might well have ceased, since Michael had completed the first-grade worktexts (Books B and C). However, Michael's parents decided that I should continue with him till the end of the school year so as to help Michael develop fluent reading of stories and books. From here on, we not only worked on the experimental drafts of the second-grade Structural Reading Series worktexts (Michael helped me to write some of the pages), but we read a number of books and also played a great many games, especially slapjack and rhyming games.

Following is a list of books Michael and I read between April 23rd and June 20th, our last lesson:

READING FOR MEANING SERIES (Boston: Houghton Mifflin Co.)

Tip by Paul McKee, Lucille Harrison, Annie McCowen, and Elizabeth Lehr. (Michael read twenty-five pages in one session, refusing to stop.)

Tip and Mitten by Paul McKee, Lucille Harrison, Annie McCowen, and Elizabeth Lehr.

The Big Show by Paul McKee, Lucille Harrison, Annie McCowen, and Elizabeth Lehr.

Up and Away by Paul McKee, Lucille Harrison, Annie McCowen, and Elizabeth Lehr.

THE HAPPY VENTURE PLAYBOOKS (London: Edinburgh, Oliver and Boyd, Ltd.)

The Happy Venture (Book 2) by Fred Schonell.

The Happy Venture (Book 3) by Fred Schonell and Phyllis Flowerdew.

THE PROSE AND POETRY SERIES (Syracuse: L. W. Singer Co.)

Story Time by Marjorie Pratt and Mary Meighen.

Story Train by Marjorie Pratt and Mary Meighen.

THE ALICE AND JERRY BASIC READERS (Evanston: Row, Peterson and Co.)

The New Wishing Well by Selma Coughlan and Mabel O'Donnell.

The New Down the River Road by Mabel O'Donnell.

NOT IN A SERIES

Easy Reading by Ellen Wales Walpole (New York: John Day Co.)

During the summer Michael read a great many books on his own. Among them were:

READING FOR MEANING SERIES (Boston: Houghton Mifflin Co.)

With Jack and Janet by Paul McKee, Lucille Harrison, Annie McCowen, and Elizabeth Lehr.

COWBOY SAM SERIES (Chicago: Benefic Press)

Cowboy Sam and Shorty by Joy Edna Walker Chandler.

Cowboy Sam and Freddy by Joy Edna Walker Chandler.

BUTTON FAMILY ADVENTURES SERIES (New York: Harcourt, Brace and World, Inc.)

The Buttons Go Camping by Edith S. McCall.

NOT IN A SERIES

The Little Red Lighthouse and the Great Gray Bridge by Hildegarde H. Swift and Lynd Ward (New York: Harcourt, Brace and World, Inc.).

In May the principal of the public school which Michael attended called me in for a conference. He knew I had been working with Michael privately. He said, "I want you to know the school is most eager to cooperate with you next year. We know Michael will be having reading lessons with you and we want to know what we should do at school. His kindergarten teacher called me in last week to observe Michael. His vision and coordination are so poor that he bumps into tables and chairs, and we are concerned about his learning to read next year." I thanked the principal but told him I would not be working with Michael after June because he already could read fluently. When I saw how surprised the principal was, I enumerated the books Michael had been reading with me and suggested that the principal might like Michael to read to him.

At the end of the teaching course, on June 18th and 19th, I gave Michael the Gates Diagnostic Tests and his scores were as follows: *

	Reading Grade	*Reading Age*
Word Recognition	3.3	8-9
Sentence Reading	2.9	8-5
Paragraph Reading	2.7	8-3

Michael finished the Word Recognition Test in ten minutes, rather than the fifteen minutes allowed, with assurance and certainty. He sounded out most of the words he didn't know correctly, except for seven words, with which he asked me for help. Those items were counted wrong in his score. He asked me out of habit; he wanted to be absolutely sure and refused to guess.

---

* "If the child's raw score equals a Reading Grade of 2.0, it means that his reading ability is equal to that of the average child at the beginning of the second grade; if the Reading Grade is 2.5, the child reads about as well as the average child at the middle of grade 2, and so on.

". . . If a child's Reading Age is 8-3 (8 years + 3 months), it means that his reading ability is approximately that of average children of that age." [3]

In the Sentence Reading Test he got thirty-eight items right out of forty-five. He read every sentence without guessing. Again the seven he missed were those with which he had asked me for help and were therefore counted wrong.

In the Paragraph Reading Test he missed six out of twenty-six; five of these items he asked for help with. Only the last item did he not understand.

To this day, Michael's success in school has been marked. He has been in the top reading group from the first grade on, and reads all sorts of books intensively, including many supposed to be several years beyond his age level. Since Michael is a very bright boy, his ability to read well and with pleasure has opened all avenues of learning to him and has sustained his success in school. There is no doubt that Michael's poor vision would have caused him great difficulty if he had been taught by the sight method. The tracing and writing of letters helped Michael to establish the form of the letters firmly in his mind. This emphasis on kinesthetic activity helped him to overcome the handicap of poor vision. But more important, with the Structural Reading method he could learn to read by relying primarily on his good intelligence, rather than his bad eyes. He learned not by sight but by insight.

The Case of Ann

Ann was one of the few children we taught who found it hard to progress from sounding words out to reading them at sight, and from reading single words to reading sentences. The following account shows the additional teaching procedures which effectively helped Ann to progress to reading mastery, procedures that should be helpful to classroom teachers faced with similar problems.

Ann was brought to me when she was only five, not because her parents anticipated that she would have difficulty in school, but because they knew about our method and wished to have their daughter taught by it. Ann had approximately two lessons a week, while she was attending a public-school kindergarten where no formal reading readiness program was taught.

Ann learned the sounds and letters in the Readiness Book in

two months. She found writing letters an exciting task and enjoyed the accompanying games, such as the Snatching Game, the Folder Game, and the Sound Lotto Game. Her skill amply demonstrated that she was ready to learn to read; she had in full measure the motivation, the ability to concentrate, and the mental equipment required. However, almost from the start, she showed one unusual inability: in order to write any letter, she had to think of the key picture to remember how the letter looked. This continued even when she had progressed to Book B. Thus, in recording *ha t,* Ann would say, "When I have to write *t* I remind myself of the tree and then I write it." Since most children taught by the Structural Reading method do not refer to the key pictures after the Readiness Book is completed, Ann's repeated return to them suggested that she had a poor visual memory. This possibility was confirmed when Ann had difficulty with recognizing known words at sight.

Ann had no difficulty, however, in advancing from reading sounds to reading words; her comments show that she was able to sound out and then read words with full comprehension.

Read	*Commented*
ma n, man	Yes, it's the picture of a man.
ca t, cat	I looked at the picture. It is a cat.
ha t, hat	To wear on your head.
ra t, rat	An animal—like a mouse.
pa n, pan	To cook things in.

After completing the first page of Book B, Ann exclaimed, "And now I can read!" Ann handled pages 2 and 3 with assurance. She liked to write the words at the bottom of the pages, and found the end sounds by recalling the shape of the key pictures. When she came to the first testing pages (pages 11, 12, 13, 14 ff.) where no pictures of the spoken words appear, she was no longer sure of how to pronounce the main parts of the words. Here I encouraged her to help herself by referring to the Picture Dictionary.

Ann found *fa* under the *fan* and, now certain of what the word said, turned back to page 11, read *fan,* and following the directions colored the fan blue.

When Ann came to the word *can* she had to look up *ca*. She found *ca* under *cat* and thus was sure it said [ca]. Turning back to the test page, she now read the word *can* without difficulty. She said, "I can read this page, but I need those pictures." Because this procedure made Ann independent of the teacher, she gained confidence in her own ability.

The following excerpts from Ann's record show her success with reading and writing single words, and the ease with which she extracted the meaning of each separate word.

October 12th. Book B page 11 (experimental copy of Book B).

	Read	*Commented*
	Can? No, ja m, jam!	It couldn't be can, it starts with [j].
October 27th	fa n, fan	You fan yourself.
	ca t, cat	You pat her, nice pussy cat.
	ca p, cap	You put it on your head.
	ba t, bat	You hit a ball with it.

November 2nd. Although Ann read all ă-words well, she was still sounding them out, so we played more than the usual number of games, such as the Word Lotto and the Snatching Game, before we advanced to sentence reading. Her speed in sounding out increased markedly. Nevertheless, she had considerable trouble reading and understanding the first sentences presented to her. Therefore, we prepared for sentence reading orally by making Ann aware of what she herself *had*—a red dress, a doll, a hat. Then, when she was asked what dad had, she was able to read *Dad has a nap, Dad has a hat,* and decide from the accompanying picture which was the correct phrase. She then completed page 17 successfully, although she often had to read a sentence twice to be sure she had understood its meaning. Not one word was misread. Some words were still sounded out, although at a much faster rate than in the beginning. She obviously needed more practice if she was to advance to sight reading. To her great delight I made a booklet for her to read, and her comments show how well she understood each sentence. To increase her interest I used the names of her brother and sisters in the sentences.

Read	Commented
Ann has a cat.	That's true.
Mike has a bat.	Yes, he does.
Linda has a bag.	Yes, she does, it's with her dress-up clothes.
Wendy has a hat.	Yes, she does.
Ann is big.	[grins] That's true.
Ann has a fan.	I do really.

November 7th. Ann's record shows that her reading was proceeding at a faster rate; the previous gap between the main part and ending of words was barely noticeable. Almost all ă-words were now read at sight; the ĭ-words could therefore be introduced.

November 13th. Ann handled pages 28, 29, and 30 of Book B without any difficulty. She continued to use the Picture Dictionary throughout the ĭ-section. (See Chapter 11, page 163.) She enjoyed the Folder Game with the ĭ-dominoes, and her comments show how well she understood how each word was built.

December 1st	Picked up domino	Commented
	si	That goes on *six.* Now I have to look for *x.*
	si	This can go on *sip.* I need a *p.*
	pi	That goes on *pig,* and I get a *g.*
	li	That's for *lid,* and there is the *d.* Gee, I love these games, I wish I could do more.

Through the domino games Ann mastered the writing of the words studied thus far. At this time, she began to be able to write some words from dictation that she had never seen.

December 7th. I dictated some ĭ-words as part of a story.

Ann wrote: *sit, rim, bib, bag, big* without hesitating at the interspersed ă-word. When I pronounced *big,* Ann looked at me. "I haven't learned that yet." She sounded it out slowly, *bi g,* and wrote it correctly.

Since Ann's auditory discrimination was good, teaching her new word groups was relatively simple. She advanced from one group to the next without difficulty, learning $\breve{a}$-words, $\breve{\imath}$-words, $\breve{o}$-words, $\breve{u}$-words, and $\breve{e}$-words. Throughout the teaching course she particularly enjoyed the domino games, which helped her learn to spell very well. She also liked the writing task at the bottom of each teaching page.

Ann particularly enjoyed reading the booklets I made for her to supplement the worktext. Since Ann dictated some of the sentences for these booklets, a few words she had not yet studied were included. These words were carefully pronounced, and Ann was shown how they were recorded. Interestingly enough, the words *the* and *but* (introduced before $\breve{u}$ was studied) were very difficult for Ann, although they occurred as many as ten times in a single book. This is another indication of her poor visual memory; most children, having understood the structure of the word *the*, recognize it easily when they see it a second time.

December 4th. New book, entitled *Ann is glad.*

Read	Commented
The cat is fat.	Maybe she is going to have kittens.
Tim is sad.	I know why he is sad, because he hasn't anybody to play with.
Sam is ill.	That's too bad.

December 17th. Ann had requested a nonsense book. We called it *Merry Christmas to Ann.*

Read	Commented
Linda wants a mop.	[Laughed] She does not want a mop.
Barby wants a pig.	[Laughed] She does *not* want a pig.
Wendy wants a log.	She does not want a log, she really does not.

April 18th. Ann started on Book C. As in Book B, Ann caught on very quickly to sounding out the words, but took a very long time to advance to fluent reading. All spring we played a great many games to help Ann master the new groups of words that ended or began with consonant blends. We purposely went very slowly in Book C, sometimes working through only one page in a lesson.

May 17th. I dictated the following words to Ann as part of a story: *lamp, pump, pond, best.* Ann did not make a single spelling mistake, yet when she read them back to me, she sounded the words out and did not read them at sight.

There were no lessons in the summer. In the fall Ann entered first grade but continued to take lessons.

I experimented to see if sentences that Ann could not comprehend when she first read them would be understood after special teaching. Book C was not yet completed, and the two pages cited below differ somewhat from the final version.

September 27th. Ann read page 18. (Words which show a gap between the main part and ending were sounded out; all others were read at sight.)

> Pa t sa ng to the cat.
> The bell ra ng and ra ng.
> Dad did not like the bi g ba ng.

When asked what each sentence meant Ann said she didn't know. We then copied the sentences on paper and cut them up in strips. I then divided a piece of paper into two columns.

Who?	What are they doing?
Jim and his gang	will take the bus

I asked Ann: "Who is the story about?" Ann found the slip saying "Jim and his gang" and we placed it in the first column. Next I asked Ann to find the slip that told what they were doing. Ann found "will take the bus" and put it in the next column. We went on with the rest of the sentences in the same way. Ann completed the sentences each time. "Can I do it all over again?" she asked enthusiastically. She shuffled the slips and reconstructed the sentences again. As she put "The bell" in the first column, I asked her, "What did the bell do?" Ann said, "It rang," and picked up the slip that read "rang and rang" without hesitation. Then we put the slips away and Ann again opened Book C to page 21. Ann read every sentence fluently this time, and talked about each one with full comprehension. Ann wanted to play the game with the sentence strips a third time. She asked me if this time she could make her own sentences. I agreed, and she changed the subjects around:

Constructed sentences	*Commented*
Pat will take the bus.	See, now I make Pat take a bus.
The bell rang and rang.	Write *with a bang* on a paper!
The bell rang and rang with a bang.	[I wrote the words, and she added them to the sentence.]

October 4th. In preparation for draft page 24 of Book C, I wrote sentences on paper slips, the subject on one slip and the predicate on the second.

Who?	What are they doing?
Jack	stands on his head.
Jill	runs down the hill.
Ted	rocks her doll. [Ann removed this slip, saying "Oh no, we can't use *her* for a boy.]
Ted	packs his bag.
Tim	runs fast.
Nell	rocks her doll.

When all the sentences were built, I asked Ann to remove the sentence which said, "Tim runs fast"; this reversal of the game proved to be of great help for speeding up Ann's reading. Although the sentences in the game had different combinations of subjects and predicates from those on the worktext page, Ann was able to read the worktext page with complete understanding. She still sounded some words out, however.

Read	*Commented*
My dog begs well.	He would go like this, on two legs.
My dog runs fast.	Well, his legs have to move fast.
Tom se lls plu ms. Tom sells plums.	Oh, he is selling plums. Where is a plum around here? They are sort of soft and nice, but I don't like them.
Ted pa cks his bag.	Where is a bag in here? There is a sort of bag and you pack things in it.

Jack wants the ball.	Here is a sort of ball, and Jack wants the ball and this is the ball that he wants.
Tim pulls his cart.	Like a wheelbarrow but you have to pull it. It's in back of you.
Jill jumps well.	Well, I could do it. [She jumps up and down to demonstrate.]

Analyzing sentences in this way is of great help in teaching children to read them. The broken-down sentences present a shorter unit to be read at a time. When the words are then placed under their respective headings, the role each word plays in building up the sentence becomes evident.

Book C was completed by February 19th. It was interesting to note that Ann preferred vocabulary pages and rhyming pages to sentence pages. However, when the Mix-Ups appeared, their humor made Ann begin to enjoy reading sentences.

In the experimental copy of Book C from which Ann was taught, the first story appeared later than it does in the published version. When Ann came to it, she read each sentence as a separate entity and was not able to grasp the coherence of the whole story. Once more, I prepared her for this new step on the oral level, but now the preparation did not have to be elaborate. I simply told her a little about the story, and then said, "Now let's read the page to find out what happened next." Ann was then able to read the whole story comprehendingly. The oral introduction provoked such interest in the continuation of the story that she no longer stopped after the first sentence, but was intent on unravelling the plot. Soon she could read stories with ease.

February 26, March 5th, March 26th. I gave Ann (6;6) the Gates Primary Reading Tests. Her scores were:

	Reading Grade	Reading Age
Word Recognition Test	3.4	8-7
Sentence Reading Test	3.4	8-7
Paragraph Reading Test	2.7	7-11

In all three tests Ann did not guess at any words. In the Word Recognition Test she got forty-two items right, reading each of the four choices exactly. She made one careless mistake and asked me for help with six words, which I then counted off her score.

In the Sentence Reading Test Ann read almost all sentences correctly, marking the corresponding pictures with certainty. She got four wrong out of forty-five.

In the Paragraph Reading Test Ann got nineteen out of twenty-six correct. She read each paragraph carefully, making two comprehension mistakes, and asking for help with five of the paragraphs, which were then counted off her score.

It is characteristic of Ann, as well as of many other children we taught, that a large percentage of the items she missed she did not read incorrectly, but when faced with a phonetically irregular word she had not yet studied and was unable to identify by sounding it out, she preferred to ask me what the word said rather than to guess at it.

Lessons were continued until June because Ann insisted that she wanted them.

March 12th. Book D was started. A few excerpts show how her reading gained momentum in the next few months, and how her study skills were developed.

May 16th. Ann read page 108 of Book D; after she finished the page I asked her, "Why was it a joke on Joe?"

Ann said, "Well, it was an envelope inside the box. Just an envelope. Danny sent it to Joe and he laughed when his mother said 'the stronger the better' because it was just a letter. But he put it on. It would look more like a present. Joe would think, 'Oh boy, a present from Danny.' That was a joke."

In the same lesson Ann read page 113 of Book D; again I questioned her.

I: Tell me what happened in the poem.
Ann: The girl—she was going to have a party at six. She got her skirt dirty and her shirt had to be fixed.
I: Is that the whole story?
Ann: She wants to clean them and she doesn't know which one is the first to fix. She should put the shirt in the washing machine and then into the drier and out it comes.
I: This is called a poem. Do you know why?
Ann: It rhymes. Skirt and shirt, girl and whirl, six and fix.

During the summer Ann's mother watched her progress from Beginner Books, some of which she had already read with me in June, to more advanced books such as *Snip, Snapp and Snurr,* and *The Big Farm, Flicka, Dicka and Ricka* and *Flicka, Ricka, Dicka, and Their New Skates* * by Maj Lindman and, later, *B is for Betsey, Eddie and His Big Deals* † by Carolyn Haywood. At the beginning of the second grade Ann was one of two children voted best readers by her class.

When the lessons were finished, Ann had not only learned to read fluently and comprehendingly, but was able to paraphrase what she had read and to answer detailed questions about it. Since Ann has a poor visual memory it would have been extremely difficult for her to learn to read well by the sight method. This carefully prepared course of teaching, however, led her in easy steps from the sounding out of words to reading texts fluently, at sight. Equally, Ann would have had difficulty with the usual phonetic approach, since she needed special help in progressing from the reading of single words to the reading of sentences and then stories.

The Case of Emily

Emily started lessons at the age of 5 years 5 months. She came regularly once a week, except for a period of three months when I saw her twice a week. Her parents sent her because her two older siblings had been my pupils and had found learning to read by the Structural Reading method pleasurable and exciting. Both these children were now reading a great deal at home and were doing very good school work, and their parents wanted Emily to have the same good start. As it turned out, Emily's lessons proved to be necessary. Emily had no trouble in catching on to the relationship between sounds and letters. Her special learning difficulties were caused by her inability to remember which way letters are oriented in space. Therefore learning to write letters proved to be hard for Emily; her left-handedness greatly contributed to her slow rate of progress in the beginning. In spite of these handicaps she learned to read and write with confidence and enjoyment.

---

* All four titles are published by Albert Whitman and Co., Chicago.
† Both published by Harcourt, Brace and World, Inc., New York.

Emily had such difficulty remembering the way things ought to go that she often reversed commas, and sometimes studied the pictures in the folders from right to left. It is interesting that for the first few weeks she could not remember how to go from my house to hers; the distance was only four blocks, but she had to make a right turn, then a left turn, and again a right turn, then a left turn. Mastering the letters in the Readiness Book was very hard for her; to become sure, she needed a great deal of practice with games on the readiness level. Indeed, the whole Readiness Book was difficult for her.

Feb. 12th. We started on the Readiness Book.

March 12th

Emily looked at the *l*—"I forgot its name." I gave her the picture dictionary and pointed to the key picture of *l* and said, "Say the name of the object."

Emily: "Ladder, oh, it's the [l]."

March 21st

Wanting to write an ŏ, she said: "I have to look it up. I forgot how to make an *o*."

Most children make reversals of *b* and *d*, or *q* and *p* (see Chapter 4), but Emily had a hard time even with those letters that do not resemble any others. Tracing the letters was a tremendous help toward learning the correct forms; nonetheless, on pages where letters had to be written free-hand, reversals occurred. It became clear that the correspondence of sound and letter must be taught to Emily, and that writing must be dropped for a time. Dominoes bearing single letters were used for some time, and were of crucial importance. Pictures of objects whose names started with different sounds were placed in front of her, and she chose the letter for each initial sound, putting the *t* on turkey, the *s* on soap, etc.

When she was ready to write, she learned to consult the key pictures and thus could work without my help, as the following comment shows.

"How do you make the *h*? . . . the *c*? . . . I just forget the [r] and [ā] but I can look it up on the page."

Having a very independent spirit, Emily enjoyed being able to work on her own. Once when I told her she could ask me as many questions as she liked she replied, "But you should try to think first."

When Emily finished the Readiness Book, she immediately asked for the "next book." I decided to let her start on Book B although she still had difficulty with writing.

The *Picture Dictionary* helped Emily immensely. When we played the Folder Game, Emily would pick up the *ma* but feel uncertain about what it said. But when she looked in the dictionary and found the *ma* under the picture of a man, she said [ma n] to herself and knew, without any doubt, that the domino said [ma]. Thus, gradually, she became surer and surer of the main parts of words. Once we started on Book B Emily learned to read with great facility as evidenced by the following excerpts from her record.

April 17th. We started on Book B.

	Read	Commented
	jar? no, ja m, jam!	You can't tell from the picture.
May 2nd	Read	Commented
	ba g, bag!	I wish you could cover these pictures up, so I could just plain read them . . . I am glad I thought of this—if I looked at the picture I might say *suitcase,* and it would be wrong. The word says *bag.*

April 25th. Emily worked on page 15, which she particularly liked. She enjoyed deliberating over which of the words stood for an object which could belong to the picture.

Read	Commented
lap	A lap wouldn't be in the car.
gas	Gas, that would be right.
rat	A rat wouldn't be in the suitcase, it would crawl around. That is funny.
gas	[Laughed] That wouldn't go in the suitcase.
cap	A cap would go.

Emily understood the structure of the ă-words so well that she wrote the following words without having read them before: *fat, mad, sad.* The only mistake she made was a reversal of the *s*.

May 15th. Emily could read sentences comprehendingly, as the following excerpts show.

Read	*Commented*
Ann ran.	Yes, she is running—she could be runing to school or to a friend's house. She would be running to school, I think, because she would look on her watch and knew she would be late.
Dan sat.	Because he was going to eat lunch and sat at the table, or because he was going to read a book, or he was waiting for someone.
Sam ran.	He was doing the same as Ann— maybe they are in the same class.
Jan sat.	Maybe she is getting her lunch too.

Emily read page 26 (see Plate 3).

Read	*Commented*
A cat.	That's the cat, not this. That's a rat. The cat is chasing the rat.
A fat cat sat.	[She drew a line to the fat cat which is sitting and explained her choice.] Because this one is fat and this one is sitting. The other one is lying down.
A fat cat sat at a rag bag.	[Drew a line] Because this is the one. The other one is sitting at a tree.

May 16th. We started on the ĭ-words.

Read	*Commented*
	Is that a nut? I can't tell from the picture.
fi g, a fig!	Thanks for letting me read, so I could find out.

May 29th. Emily read page 40.

Read	Commented
fi sh, fish	That's a new word. I haven't had *fish,* I've only had *fin.*
i t, it	[Sounded out by herself] Well, I just read it. You could fill a bowl, you could fill *it* to the top.

June 18th. Emily read page 58.

Read	Commented
rock, dock, sock, lock	Hey, that's neat. *Dock, sock, lock, rock;* they all rhyme, because they almost sound the same. These all have the same three letters at the end, but it does not have to be three letters, it can be two like: sip and tip top and hop hot and pot

Emily read page 60 during the same lesson.

Read	Commented
[Looked at dog] dog	Dalmatian, but you couldn't fit Dalmatian in here; the word starts with *do,* so it couldn't be Dalmatian, it has to be *dog.*

September 13th. Emily tackled page 76.

Read	Commented
Can a rat live in a pan?	No, it has to have cheese.
Can an ox live in a pan?	The ox would be a little too big. It wouldn't fit in an ordinary pan.
Can a fish live on a hill?	[Laughed] Oh no, it cannot.

Emily read pages 78 and 79 during the same lesson.

Read	*Commented*
Is Bob in the pot?	That's pretty silly. They don't want to cook their own child. Well, it may have been a witch.

Sept. 19th, page 82.

Read	*Commented*
Peanut?	[Guessed from picture] Oh, it's not a peanut yet, it has to grow. The word says *nut*.
nut	
sap?	[Guessed from picture at first] It's a gun. I read it now. Something that you shoot with and boys like to play with it.
gun	
pup	Oh, I thought it was a dog from the picture, but it says *pup*.

October 3rd

Read	*Commented*
tug	[Looked at picture first] I don't know whether it's a boat or a tug. Oh, I can tell from the words: *hug* or *tug*. It's a *tug*.

In learning to spell, the dominoes were a great help to Emily, because she could build words without stumbling over the mechanics of forming letters. When building words with dominoes she learned to read each word as soon as she had built it to make sure she was correct.

Folder Game with Dominoes:

Built	*Commented*
ma n	I built *man,* not *map* which has a *p*.
ba? ba! bag	I'll use it for *bag*. Where is the *g*?
pa, pan	I'll use it for *pan*.
ra? ra? rat!	Oh, I can use it for *rat*. I need a *t*.

Emily learned to write correctly; when, as she sometimes did, she made a spelling mistake, she detected it herself by reading the word she had written.

May 16th	*Wrote*	*Corrected with comments*
	pib	I know why that's wrong. It says *pib*.
	pig	[She erases the *b*] There, I wrote *g*, now it says *pig*.
	sib	No, that says *sib*. [She erased the *b*
	sip	and wrote *p*.] Okay, now it says *sip*.
	lib	Oh no, that's a *b*, I want a *d*.
	lid	[Checked with the picture dictionary. Wrote *d*] Now it says li*d*.
June 18th		
	bo	That doesn't say *box*, I need an *x*.
	sos	Oh no, not an *s*. I don't want it. I
	sock	want it to say *sock*. [She erased *s* and wrote *ck* instead.] There, it says *sock*.
	gun	Oh, that's wrong. I want it to say
	gum	*gum*. That's it.

A sample of her written work (see Fig. 12.1) shows that at the age of 5 years and eleven months Emily was able to write down with considerable accuracy words that were dictated to her. Her only mistakes were to use capitals where they were not needed. One can still see from one erasure that she originally wrote *d* for *b*.

In thirty-eight lessons, Emily finished Book B, the red booklets which supplement Book B * and about one third of Book C.

To obtain an objective evaluation of Emily's ability, I gave her the Gates Word Recognition Test and Sentence Test. To prepare her for taking these tests before she had completed the first-grade program,† I spent one lesson showing her page 62 of

---

* There are ten supplementary booklets for Book B, and ten for Book C.

† Emily was still working in Book C when this chapter was in preparation, but we wanted to include her case to show how her tendency to reverse letters was overcome. To make her record complete, we decided to test her even though she had not yet completed the first-grade course.

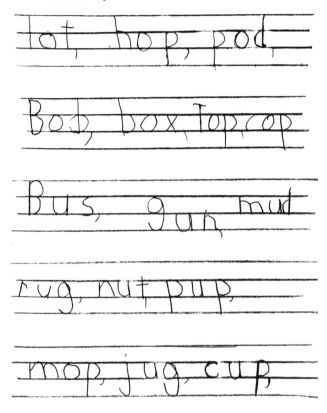

Fig. 12.1

Book C and explained the role of the magic *e*. I then let her look at the teaching pages for *ā*, *ī*, *ō* and *ū*. During the tests, Emily had to sound out the long-vowel words, which slowed her reading speed. I decided, therefore, not to keep her to the time limit, and she took about twice the permitted time. Hence, although her scores clearly indicate her superior reading ability, they cannot be considered comparable scores.

	Reading Grade	*Reading Age*
Word Recognition Test	2.9	8-5
Sentence Reading Test	2.6	8-1

Emily's attitude toward the test was very interesting. She insisted on asking my help when sounding out did not yield the correct word and became very upset when I told her to try to figure it out by herself. She said repeatedly, "Why can't you help me? I want to know what the word says." Actually, she was extremely good at figuring out new words and correcting her first inadequate pronunciation. Emily expressed great delight when she came across words she knew. "This says this dress is black. It's not that one" (pointing to a white one).

It is interesting to look at a sample list of the words Emily could not figure out, and a sample of those she could sound out.

Words she could not figure out: knife (she became angry because she pronounced the *k* and thus the word made no sense), angry, root, paint, mail, climb (she became angry about the *b*), whistle, anyway, soldier, journey, queen, roses.

New words she deciphered by sounding them out: child, softly, fairy, family, start, potato, wagon, river, pressing, music, arm, roof, wood-cutting, handkerchief, berries, factory.

It is clear from Emily's present performance that she is well on her way to becoming an excellent reader.

To be able to gauge Emily's ability to read simple books, even though she had not yet finished Book C, I let her read a hardcover book at the end of each lesson. Emily started reading Beginner Books with great pleasure and had no trouble in reading afterwards other books appealing to her interest. She figured out many unknown words by herself. She asked me for help only on those few words she could not decipher. Following is a list of the books that she read:

BEGINNER BOOKS (New York: Random House, Inc.)

Green Eggs and Ham by Dr. Seuss
Go Dog Go by P. D. Eastman
Put Me in the Zoo by Robert Lopshire
Are You My Mother? by P. D. Eastman
Dr. Seuss's ABC
Snow by Roy McKie and P. D. Eastman
The Big Honey Hunt by Stanley and Janice Berenstain

LET'S FIND OUT SERIES (New York: Franklin Watts, Inc.)

Let's Find Out About Animal Homes by Martha and Charles Shapp

Let's Find Out About Homes by Martha and Charles Shapp
Let's Find Out About Indians by Martha and Charles Shapp
Let's Find Out About the United Nations by Martha and Charles
   Shapp

Most children will be able to read and enjoy books of this kind
after they have completed Book C. Some will be able to read
them when they are halfway through Book C.

In Emily's case it was important to go slowly and not to rush
her through the letters. Emily benefited from the kinesthetic activities, which helped her to remember the forms of the letters.
She also enjoyed discovering things herself and thinking things
through rather than asking for help. Since her intelligence was
challenged, and we did not depend on her visual memory, she
could progress at a gratifying rate. Not once did Emily experience any failure; instead she found learning to read and write
an exciting adventure.

The Case of Tommy

I knew Tommy first at the age of 4; he went to nursery school
with one of my children. I had observed him with delight both
at nursery school and at birthday parties. He was a bright, in-
quisitive child, and, to my casual eye, seemed well satisfied with
the world and himself. Tommy's mother called me in February
1963 after Tommy had been in first grade for four months. She
asked me to see him professionally, because he was having difficulties in learning to read and was very upset about it; he was
irritable at home, complained that he couldn't learn to read,
and did not want to go to school any more. His mother added
that both she and her husband had been trying hard to reassure
Tommy but to no avail.

On further questioning, his mother explained that Tommy
had been reading to them. He consistently misread such words
as *apple* for *pear, dad* for *father,* and so on. Both parents had
gone to see Tommy's teacher to tell her how upset Tommy
seemed and to ask for her help. Specifically, they asked if Tommy
couldn't be given some phonics, but his teacher refused, insisting
that Tommy did not need any extra help. She assured Tommy's

parents that there was nothing to worry about. Tommy was, in fact, in the first reading group.

When Tommy came for his first lesson, March 16, 1963, I couldn't believe this was the same boy I had known two years before. He looked very solemn. His cheerful smile had disappeared, he greeted me with downcast eyes, and spoke in a high-pitched voice. As soon as a pleasant relationship was established and he had lost his shyness (in the third lesson), I gave him the Gates Word Recognition Test, telling him that it did not matter whether or not he could read all the words. We spent the rest of the hour playing the Folder Game with the ă-dominoes, and Tommy seemed to be enjoying himself. In later lessons I gave Tommy the Sentence and Paragraph tests, each time spending the rest of his lesson playing games.

Tommy was six years and eleven months old when he took the tests. His scores on the Gates Primary Reading Test (Type PWR) were as follows:

Reading Grade:	2.11
Reading Age	7-3

Since these scores seemed amazingly high, it seemed interesting to look up Tommy's percentile score. These scores placed Tommy in the 67th percentile, which means that he had performed better than 67 percent of the pupils of the same grade level on which the test scores are based.

Clearly, Tommy's reading skill was not only adequate but higher than the statistical average for his age and school grade. Yet, equally clearly, he was greatly distressed about learning to read. What was the matter? Actually, the *kind of mistakes* Tommy made on the test were highly significant; there was no question that his answers were guesses, some shrewd, some wild. A sample of these errors is listed below.

In each test item on the Gates Test there is a picture; the child selects from four words the one that fits the picture.

Word which fits picture	*Word Tommy selected*
sleep	sleds
floor	flower
letter	lettuce
penny	pencil
church	check

Word which fits picture	*Word Tommy selected*
family	softly
fruit	suit
turkey	turtle
farm	from
star	rats
potato	tomato
pan	paint
take	rake
sheep	shine
stand	band
brick	bridge
neck	check
wigwam	waves
soap	rope
cover	cocoa
lamb	land
word	wood

While he was taking the test, Tommy frequently said the name of the picture aloud; he always named it correctly, but often selected the wrong word. The words *turkey* and *turtle* have the same beginnings, as do *sleep* and *sled, floor* and *flower;* the words *fruit* and *suit* look somewhat alike; fami*ly* and soft*ly* have the same endings. Looking at the word *rats* from right to left, one reads *star*. What Tommy needed were serviceable tools which he could use to unlock words. His errors were the result of the reading instruction he was given at school. According to his percentile score on the Gates Test, 67 percent of his peers throughout the country may be in the same predicament!

April 6th. I gave Tommy the Sentence Reading Test. His scores were:

Reading Grade:	1.7
Reading Age:	6-11

Again, he made the same kind of mistakes. He looked at the word *balloon,* but marked the picture of the butterfly; because he often guessed right, his score does not reflect his inability to read.

After Tommy had had eight lessons, on April 27th, I gave Tommy the Paragraph Reading Test. He showed a distinct change in attitude; when he did not know a word, which happened most of the time, he refused to guess. He tried to sound out each word, but he asked me to help him whenever he could not figure a word out. In this score, I did not count anything right that I helped him with.

Tommy's scores on this test were:

Reading Grade:	2.1
Reading Age:	7-3

This time Tommy was not so unhappy about taking the test, but he was glad when it was over, and he could return to the worktext.

April 27th

Tommy commented as I opened Book B: "Good, we go on with the book." I asked him if he liked the book. Tommy: "I like this book better. I guess I like it better if I can read the words. You figure out what the words sound like."

During the following lessons Tommy occasionally looked at a picture first, as he was taught to do in school, and guessed what word it might stand for. But then he always sounded the word out and corrected himself.

Said	Read	Commented
truck?	va n	A van! I figured it out.
book?	pa d	A pad!
Dad?	Da n	Dan! A boy's name!

Occasionally Tommy was unsure about the main part of some word. He looked at the word *pack* and being uncertain, looked *pa* up in the Picture Dictionary. There he found *pa* under the picture of a *pan;* he said "pa," turned back to the worktext page and read with confidence: "pa ck, pack!" The Picture Dictionary was of decisive help in reteaching Tommy. It did a great deal to develop his confidence in his growing reading ability and it gave him the feeling of achievement.

May 3rd. Tommy started on the ĭ-words; he experienced no difficulties with this new step.

When Tommy read page 29 he looked at the picture. "I can't tell from the picture because it looks just like a plain, old fish. But the word—it does not have a *sh* sound but an *n* at the end, so it's not fish. Wait—it's fi n, it's *fin!*"

Tommy tackled page 43. "It can't be plate because it starts with *di* . . . di sh, it's a dish!" Added of his own volition: "I am better at school, because I know the sounds. When I don't know a word, I just sound it out and then I know it."

May 10th. Tommy read page 68 with the help of the Picture Dictionary in front of him.

"Hm, the rat *is* on top of the cat" (checking with picture after he had read the sentence).

"I wouldn't like to be the fox. He might get hurt. The ox might hurt him with his horns."

Later, he said, "In school they didn't teach me the sounds. Tony learned in nursery school and he told us."

May 18th. Tommy read the poem on page 74 so well that I tested his comprehension.

I: What's the very last thing he passes on his way back?
Tommy: The mill.
I: What is the very first thing he passes?
Tommy: The mill—because he started there and he finished there.

In the same lesson he read page 76.

Read *live* without help.
I: How do you know this word?
Tommy: I sounded it out.

June 1st. Tommy read *bun* and *hut* by transfer. In the same lesson he did page 87.

When he saw the picture of a boat he guessed it was a ship. *"Ship?"* Tommy said to himself, "that wouldn't fit. *Tu g, it's a tug.*"

June 20th. Page 93.

"You know how I did it. I sounded it out (*bu g*) and then you can write it."
Pointed to *muff* and *puff*. "I haven't had these two words." I encouraged him to try to sound them out. *"Mu ff* and *pu ff, muff* and *puff,* that's easy."

June 22nd

Read "Peg is sick in bed" in a critical voice. "You should have drawn a girl sick in bed."

"I am glad I am having reading lessons. They are fun. My sister (age five) should come here."

June 25th. Tommy started on Book C. He had completed Book B in fifteen lessons.

For a month Tommy improved steadily in both reading and writing; every lesson showed that Tommy now mistrusted pictures, knowing they could not tell him exactly what word was meant. He comprehended sentences and stories so well that he felt free to criticize the pictures, and ceased entirely using them as clues.

Besides the picture dictionary, the domino games were the greatest help for Tommy with spelling, particularly when two vowel groups were mixed up. We also played the Sorting Games very often, although Tommy was only willing to play games after he had read a minimum of 8 pages. A few more excerpts will further illustrate Tommy's progress.

July 17th. Tommy read pages 26, 27, 28 of Book C.

My questions	*Tommy's answers*
Did Peg have a baby sister?	Yes.
What did Peg lose?	A ring.
Did Peg have a brother?	The story does not tell.
Where was the ring?	In the sink at the gas station.

When Tommy read page 46 of Book C he commented:

"The king is in the pig pen. . . . That's the funniest because you usually don't see a king in a pig pen."

He enjoyed the Fix-Ups:

"I know where the pig is—in the pig pen. I like this game. The king is at his desk. That's where he really is."

September 13th. Tommy returned after a month's vacation. He had entered second grade in school and reported excitedly as he came into the study:

"I am at the top of my class. I can read *Down the River Road.* It's harder than all the other books. I sound out the new words."

September 18th. Tommy had just finished reading page 60, and I asked him to tell me in his own words what he read.

"Oh, you see, the witch was lying down and put her lunch on the stump, and the fox came along to take it, but the witch looked up and saw the fox. She said, 'Stop!' but he didn't. Then she cast a spell on the fox to make him into a frog, and then he was little and had to leave her lunch. And he went away."

At the end of the lesson Tommy peeked at my notes, and laughed: "I can read a lot. There, that says *spin!*"

Because Tommy had learned the alphabet names of the letters first, instead of the *sounds* that letters represent, he had considerable trouble building the words he read with the dominoes and found it very hard to write these words at self-dictation. He could say [ba g], could write *ba*, but when he wanted to write [g], he did not know what letter to use. Similarly, he could dictate [ma t] to himself and write *ma* correctly, but did not know by what letter to record the [t] that he heard at the end. Having learned the name *tee* at school, he did not know that it recorded the sound of [t].

Tommy understood the difference between the sound-names and the alphabet-names of letters when I pointed it out to him, and we went through the Readiness Book at this point so he could learn the sound-names. He was delighted to find the key pictures, which enabled him to work independently, and he studied the sound-names eagerly. He soon gained so much confidence in his ability to write words on his own that he asked me to cover up the top of page 39 of Book B when he came to the writing task.

Throughout the remainder of the teaching course Tommy asked to have the top parts of teaching pages covered up because he could write the words. The following excerpts show how rapidly he gained skill in writing words correctly.

May 5th. Tommy worked on page 55 of Book B.

Wrote	Commented
dot	I know what is at the end because I can hear the [t].
rod	I can write it. I hear what's at the end, a [d].
a rock	A sharp [k] sound at the end, so you write *ck* like in sick.

His answers to the Mix-Ups on page 47 of Book C, which he wrote without help, are included here as a sample of his writing. (See Fig. 12.2.) The second sample was written from dictation. (See Fig. 12.3.) On rereading the sentences, he found and corrected his mistakes himself.

When Tommy finished Book C and had started on Book D, I again gave him the Gates Tests using Form 2 instead of Form 1. This time the tests were a challenge he enjoyed meeting, and he

The pig is in the

pig pen.

The king is at his

desk.

The drum is on the

band stand.

Fig. 12.2

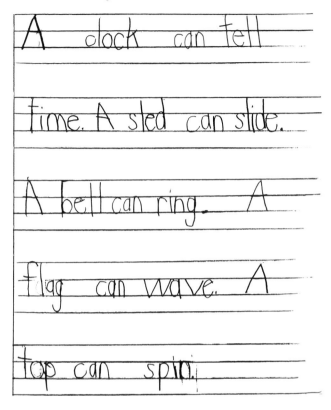

A clock can tell time. A sled can slide. A bell can ring. A flag can wave. A top can spin.

Fig. 12.3

proceeded with confidence. Tommy's scores on the three tests were as follows:

Tommy (7;8)	Reading Grade	Reading Age
Word Recognition Test	3.5	8-9
Sentence Reading Test	3.4	8-11
Paragraph Reading Test	3.2	8-8

Again Tommy's scores are not as significant as the quality of his performance. In the Word Recognition Test he worked rapidly and with confidence, completing the test in six minutes instead of the allotted fifteen, and did not make a single mistake.

He finished the Sentence Reading Test in nine minutes, and again did not make a single mistake.

In the Paragraph Reading Test, he finished in nine minutes, making three mistakes. The first was careless: he read the paragraph comprehendingly but did not carry out the directions properly. The other two items, 23 and 26, required that he visualize how to draw a line on the maps that appeared. He could not do this. Children often find these two items difficult, so we have included similar maps and tasks in books D and E. However, Tommy had not reached them when he took the tests.

It was gratifying to see Tommy regain his confidence. He now feels that he really belongs in that first reading group, to which he had been assigned because he often guessed correctly. He often reports that he had figured out a word in class which his peers could not decipher.

Tommy was taught to read in eleven months at the rate of one lesson a week. Fortunately for him, his remedial work took place at the beginning of his school career, so his despair was of short duration.

BIBLIOGRAPHICAL NOTES

1. CATHERINE STERN AND TONI S. GOULD, *The Early Years of Childhood, Education Through Insight* (New York: Harper and Brothers, 1955), p. 183.

2. KURT LEWIN, *A Dynamic Theory of Personality* (New York: McGraw-Hill Book Co., 1935).

3. ARTHUR I. GATES, *Manual for the Gates Primary Reading Tests* (New York: Teachers College, Columbia University, 1958), p. 8.

Summary

Perhaps the greatest single achievement of the Structural Reading method is the focusing of children's interest on the learning process itself. Although starting with sounds may seem somewhat pedestrian to adults, it is by no means devoid of interest to children themselves. But even more, when children come to learn how to decipher words, they are fascinated. Now the business of learning to read comes alive and becomes challenging and productive in itself. Children find every step of the learning process intelligible, and each one progresses with an ever-increasing confidence and pride in his ability.

At various times in the history of education, it has been considered expedient to capture children's interest in order to enlist it in the learning process. The followers of progressive education have consistently emphasized the necessity of making subject matter interesting and meaningful. They rightly rejected the old alphabet method of teaching reading, with its lifeless drill of letters and of piecemeal blending of sounds, since this kind of instruction made no effort to make itself interesting. Too often, however, the principles of progressive education have been misunderstood, and children's interests have been blindly followed. As Richard Hofstadter has said, "Remarkably effective beginnings were made at mobilizing the child's interest for learning, but often these interests simply displaced learning." [1]

As the alphabet method of teaching reading was gradually abandoned, the sight method or whole-word method took over, and, indeed, the whole-word method did seem to be geared to children's interests. What was overlooked was that it neither fits the structure of the language nor directs that interest to the salient point of the reading process. It is true that almost every child is interested in the working of a gas station or a post office or a fire house. However, when an attempt is made to use this interest as a motivation for learning to read, it is found that it remains focused on the exciting events, and it is rarely transferred to the chore of memorizing the shape of the words. It is the teacher and not the class who reads the words that describe an experience; the pupils only try hard to remember which word she has attached to each of a series of total configurations.

In the Structural Reading method, in contrast, children actively discover reading for themselves. The comments of our pupils show a real interest in learning to read, and prove at the same time that the vitality of the classroom is enhanced, not threatened by, this new approach to the teaching of reading.

To make Structural Reading a sound, effective program, it must be supplemented by the activities which have become part of the modern classroom, activities which enlarge children's backgrounds and enrich their vocabularies. Trips, large picture charts, pictures from the first worktext, and whatever other pictorial help a teacher can devise, all serve to stimulate lively class discussions. But the experiences are not used directly for teaching reading. Rather, when a child has learned to read the word *gas* in the worktext, all that he knows about gas stations will come to his mind, and he will want to share his knowledge with the class. It is in the stimulation of this meaningful kind of experience that trips and pictures have their useful function. Every word actually read by a child, from the first pages of the worktext on, will start him talking about his experiences.

Later, when the pupils are well on their way to reading and writing, experience charts may be composed by the teacher and the class together, to keep a record of interesting events. Experience charts should not be used to teach words to the beginning reader; they must be postponed until children are actually able to read them without help.

As the facility in reading grows, reading will have become as natural as talking, so that the children's interest is now centered on the content of the story they are reading. At the end of first grade, most children taught by the Structural Reading method are able to read beginner books themselves. The relatively slow beginning, made by teaching sounds, is more than compensated for later on by amazing growth of children's reading vocabularies. At each level, the vocabulary our pupils command is much larger than any list of sight words in any basal reader.

The true achievement of our method, however, is not to be measured by the number of single words our pupils can read, but by the astonishing frequency with which they transfer their knowledge to reading new words successfully. To start reading with a list of sight words is wrong on two counts: first, it eliminates all possibility of transfer; and second, it permits guessing, a habit that must be unlearned later. In contrast, in the Structural Reading method, the words a child is not yet able to read at a glance, he is able to sound out; moreover, most new words can be figured out by transfer, which is a direct result of teaching by giving children insight into structural relations. We have shown how the student is led, step by step, from the structure of spoken and printed words to the sentence, the paragraph, and the story. He not only learns to read and write, but by grasping the structural characteristics of spelling and by learning simple grammatical concepts, he is led to an ever-deepening insight into the structure of the language. The pupil is thus prepared for the increasingly more complex study of the English language that he will meet in the higher grades. In this respect, Structural Reading duplicates modern instruction in mathematics and science. As Jerome Bruner has pointed out, "Various people who have worked on curricula in science and mathematics have urged that it is possible to present the fundamental structure of a discipline in such a way as to preserve some of the exciting sequences that lead a student to discover for himself." [2]

Working with the Structural Reading method, not only is the child spared frustration and permitted to enjoy learning to read, but the teacher, too, finds consistent success where she has hitherto found frequent failure. She becomes more confident and not only can expect to do more for her pupils but can expect more from them. "More and more we are coming to see," says John Gardner, "that high performance, particularly where children are concerned, takes place in a framework of expectation. If it is expected it will often occur. If there are no expectations, there will be little high performance. . . . High individual performance will depend to some extent on the capacity of the society or institution to evoke it. And woe to the society that loses the gift for such evocation! When an institution, organization or nation loses its capacity to evoke high individual performance, its great days are over." [3]

Although no method can make a slow child move as fast or as far as a superior one, our experience demonstrates that Structural Reading helps even slow children from failure to success in reading. Teachers do justice to all children only when they help each child to develop his intellect to its fullest capacity. When teachers do this they are functioning at their best, as teachers and as human beings. In the words of Phillip Brooks, which we found on the opening page of a first reader published in 1901: "He who helps a child helps humanity with a distinctness, with an immediateness, which no other help given to human creatures in any stage of their human life can possibly give again."

BIBLIOGRAPHICAL NOTES

1. RICHARD HOFSTADTER, *Anti-intellectualism in American Life* (New York: Alfred A. Knopf, 1963), p. 375.

2. JEROME S. BRUNER, *The Process of Education* (New York: Vintage Books, 1963), p. 9.

3. JOHN GARDNER, *Excellence, Can We Be Equal and Excellent Too?* (New York: Harper and Brothers, 1961), pp. 101, 96.

Index

Accuracy, in reading, 21, 65, 66, 70, 75, 77, 127, 129; *see also* Guessing
Achievement, intellectual, 3, 13, 30, 31, 37, 55, 68, 89, 150, 151, 155, 178, 212, 219, 221, 222; *see also* Intelligence; Success; Thinking
Alphabet, 7, 8; *see also* Letters
Apostrophe, use of, 111-13
Association
 of letters and sounds, 7, 8; *see also* Correspondence, of letters and sounds; Memorization
 of words and meaning, 10, 11, 12
Associative bonds, 5
Auditory discrimination; *see* Discrimination

Barnhart, Clarence L., 14
Barzun, Jacques, 6
Betts, Emmet A., 36
Blending, 7, 9, 30, 35, 59, 219
Blends, ready-made, 30, 59; *see also* Consonant blends
Bloomfield, Leonard, 9, 34
Bonds; *see* Associative bonds
Books, 53, 56, 87-8, 89, 156, 179, 188-90, 200, 208, 209
Bruner, Jerome S., 6, 28, 51, 108, 151, 155, 221

Case studies, 185-218
Castle School, 48, 50, 151, 152, 178
Children
 culturally deprived, 153, 179-82; *see also* Test results
 gifted, 51, 151, 153, 222
 slow, 43, 44, 51, 84, 85, 153, 222
Chinese language, 8, 10
Clues; *see* Word recognition
Comprehension, 25, 30, 34, 54, 59, 67, 68, 72, 74, 76, 78, 80, 84, 98, 101, 192, 196; *see also* Insight; Structural Reading
Conant, James B., 13
Confidence, 25, 27, 31, 33, 35, 54, 61, 87, 118, 121, 155, 160, 179, 184, 186, 193, 212, 215, 217, 218, 219, 221

Configuration, 10, 17, 20, 21, 150, 151, 220; *see also* Words, shape of
Consonant blends
 final, 95
 initial, 97
Consonants, 47, 57, 63, 177
Content, 7, 81, 139, 220
Correspondence, of letters and sounds, 9, 29, 42, 51, 55, 60, 90, 154, 155, 158, 159, 200
Context, 10, 20, 21, 68, 69, 86, 126
 clues from, 8, 21
Cremin, Lawrence A., 3
Culturally deprived children; *see* Children
Curiosity, 26, 50

Dewey, John, 149
Differences, individual, 152, 156
Digraphs, 120
Diphthongs, 103
Discovery, 5, 6, 28 ff., 32, 35 ff., 52, 54, 56, 59, 66, 86, 94, 102, 113, 150 ff., 153, 155, 209, 220
Discrimination
 Auditory, 41, 42, 43, 44, 154, 194; *see also* Games
 Visual, 41, 154, 155, 191 ff., 195, 200
Dolch, Edward W., 36, 44, 152
Doman, Glenn, 151
Dominoes, 59, 60, 92, 97, 98, 100, 165-8, 171, 177, 186, 195, 201, 205, 214
Drawings; *see* Functional drawings
Durell, Donald D., 154
Durkin, Dolores, 51, 127, 150, 151
Drill, 5, 7, 15, 35, 41, 61
D'Rilly Alphabet, 15, 17, 18, 22-7

Education, 3, 149, 155, 219
Errors, 61, 74, 75, 93-4, 98, 129, 206, 210, 211
Excellence, 150
Experience chart, 17, 55, 56, 78, 220

Failure, 12, 13, 36, 55, 183, 184, 185, 209
Fluency; *see* Reading, at sight; Structural Reading

Foundation, 55, 87, 127, 143, 184
Fries, Charles C., 30
Functional drawings, 108, 113, 116, 120

Games, 152, 155, 158-77; *see also* Dominoes
rhyming, 94
to teach auditory discrimination, 42, 43, 47
writing, 62, 63, 168, 177, 185, 186
Gans, Roma, 19
Gardner, John, 221, 222
Gates, Arthur I., 20, 36, 128, 129
Gates Primary Reading Tests, 178, 181, 190
results of, 178, 190, 198, 199, 207, 210, 211, 212, 217, 218
Gestalt psychology, 10
Gifted children; *see* Children
Grammatical concepts, 88-9, 107, 109, 126, 221
Gray, William S., 36
Guessing, 10, 21, 68, 75, 77, 128, 129, 177, 184, 190, 210, 212, 221

Hall, Robert A., 29, 42
Havighurst, R. J., 51
Hofstadter, Richard, 150, 219

Ideograph, 8, 10
Imagination, 68, 77, 81
Individualized reading instruction, 87-8, 152
Inflection; *see* Root words
Initial sounds; *see* Sounds, initial
Insight, 4-7, 10-12, 21, 24, 28, 30, 31, 35, 36, 47, 54, 57, 61, 66, 67, 84, 91, 108, 153, 191, 221
Intelligence, 7, 13, 37, 45, 54, 68, 209; *see also* Achievement
Interest, 8, 17, 27, 37, 45, 51, 62, 87, 88, 128, 149, 150, 179, 193, 219, 220
Intonation, 64, 70, 85
Iowa Tests of basic skills, 128, 131

Key pictures, 29, 45, 154, 158, 192, 201, 215
Kindergarten, 41, 50, 51, 151, 190; *see also* Pre-reading program
Kinesthetic experience, 49, 191, 209
Koehler, Wolfgang, 4

Language arts program, 36, 157
Learning, 4-13, 16, 19, 26, 27, 37, 61, 66, 219; *see also* Insight
to listen, 29, 33, 41, 45, 51, 61
to read, 4, 15-27, 28-37, 52, 209, 221
Left-right direction, 20, 35, 45, 94
Letters
alphabet names of, 44, 45, 99, 162, 184, 215
role of, 12, 47
sound names of, 44, 45, 167, 215; *see also* Correspondence, of letters and sounds
Lewin, Kurt, 184
Linguists, 9, 29, 30, 34, 42

Magic E, function of, 87, 99-103, 207
Main word part; *see* Words, parts of
Mastery, 6, 11, 36, 127
Maturation, 41, 51, 52
McKee, Paul, 9, 15
Meaning, 7, 9, 10, 12, 21, 25, 28, 30 ff., 64, 67, 69, 70, 74, 77, 83-4, 117, 129, 193
Meaningful whole, 10, 28
Mechanics of reading; *see* Reading, mechanics of
Memorization, 4, 5, 6, 8, 12, 19, 20, 21, 22, 26, 28, 42, 51, 55, 90, 92, 108, 122, 150, 151; *see also* Association, of letters and sounds
Mode of attack, 5, 19, 22, 30, 31, 36, 129
Monosyllabic words; *see* Words, monosyllabic
Motivation, 17, 26, 220

New York City Board of Education, 145
New York Tests of Growth in Reading, 180

Oral introduction to new steps, 72, 81, 97, 99, 108, 139, 143, 195, 198; *see also* Pre-reading program
Orton, Samuel T., 49, 155

Phonic clues; *see* Word recognition, clues to
Phonics approach, 7-9, 11, 12, 30, 66, 70, 149, 150, 219

Phonograms, 9, 11, 35, 95
Picture clues; *see* Word recognition, clues to
Picture Dictionary, 61, 155, 158, 159, 163, 164, 165, 185, 186, 192 202, 212
Pictures, 10, 20, 21, 30, 31, 44, 56, 57, 58, 60, 63, 67, 108, 135, 153, 160, 212, 214; *see also* Key pictures
Plurals, formation of, 108-10, 123
Practice, 32, 33, 62, 65, 66, 75, 76, 87, 95, 152, 159, 165
Prefixes, 116, 118
Pre-primers, 18, 26, 55
Pre-reading program, 42-52; *see also* Structural Reading Series, Book A; Kindergarten
Primers, 9, 18, 20, 26, 27, 74, 86
Pronunciation, 44, 104, 113, 114, 118, 120, 121, 129, 154, 160, 179
development of correct, 154, 160, 185

Reader, expert, 7, 10, 11, 85
Readiness Book; *see* Pre-reading program; Reading readiness; Structural Reading Series, Book A
Reading, 9, 12, 33, 36, 86; *see also* Learning; Letters; Oral introduction to new steps; Sentences; Structural Reading; Vocabulary; Words
at sight, 17, 22, 26, 32, 65, 66, 70, 94, 127, 128, 170, 173, 186-8, 193-8, 200
beginning instruction of, 36, 55
explosion, 86
mechanics of, 7, 36, 81
oral, 84-5
process of, 7, 26, 27, 36, 72
silent, 84-5
teaching of, 6, 7, 8, 10, 11, 13, 26, 27, 31, 51
Reading readiness, 18, 41, 42, 44; *see also* Pre-reading program
Related reading skills, 36, 88, 128, 129-44
Remedial work, 21, 22, 113, 115, 122, 128, 129, 165, 177, 182, 183, 184, 218

Rereading, 136, 138
Retention, 6, 36
Reversals, 20, 49, 50, 201, 206
Root words, inflection of, 113 ff., 118
Rules, 107 ff., 113
Russell, David H., 36, 143

Self-dictation, 59, 91, 92, 102, 215; *see also* Spelling
Self-reliance, 37, 62
Sentences
illustrating, 78, 80-1
learning to read, 32, 66-7, 69-80, 188, 193
role of, 33
writing, 78
Shapp, Charles M., 179, 208. 209
Sight approach, 7-8, 9-12, 15-19, 21-2, 26, 32, 55, 68, 70, 74, 90, 129, 150, 151, 183, 184, 191, 200, 219, 220
Sight vocabulary, 18, 26, 31, 36, 56, 66; *see also* Vocabulary
Silent E; *see* Magic E
Skill, 127
of following printed directions, 129
of map reading, 131, 138
of noting details, 134
of reading to appreciate general significance, 129, 139
Slow children; *see* Children
Smith, Nila B., 128, 129
Sound Book, 48, 156, 163
Sound Picture Cards, 161, 162
Sounding out, 20, 30, 32, 33, 34, 36, 61, 75, 86-7, 94, 191, 193, 195, 196, 212, 214, 221; *see also* Structural Reading
Sounds; *see also* Correspondence, of letters and sounds
function of, 12, 29
initial, 29, 42-50, 154, 159, 179
role of, 10
Spalding, Romana B., 55
Speaking vocabulary; *see* Vocabulary, speaking
Speech defects, correction of, 44, 154
Spelling, 22, 25, 33, 54, 61, 90-4, 102, 103, 104, 105, 144, 205, 221; *see also* Self-dictation

Spoken words; *see* Words

Stern, Catherine, 5, 15

Stone, Joseph L., 153

Stories, learning to read, 80, 83-6

Story telling, 41, 80-1, 154

Structural analysis, 20, 25, 35; *see also* Sounding out

Structural arithmetic, 5, 28

Structural characteristics, 28, 36, 102, 115, 123, 149

Structural Reading, 28, 30, 33, 34 ff., 51-2, 55-68, 89, 91, 96, 108, 126, 152, 221; *see also* Sounding out

Structural Reading Series

Book A, "We Learn to Listen" (Readiness Book), 29, 44-7, 153-4, 156, 185, 186, 191-2, 201-2, 215

Book B, "We Discover Reading," 30, 56, 58, 60, 62, 66, 72, 77, 83, 85, 125, 130, 135, 155, 156, 164, 165, 188, 192, 202, 206, 215

Book C, "We Read and Write," 87, 99, 112, 130, 135, 156, 170, 178-9, 187, 206, 214, 216

Book D, "We Read More and More," 99, 110, 113 ff., 119, 125, 131, 132, 136, 139, 140

Book E, "Now We Read Everything," 125, 131, 137-9, 141-3

Supplementary booklets, 80, 156, 206

Structure, 5, 6, 28, 31, 32, 35, 57, 102

of the language, 7, 8, 12, 220

of phonetically regular words, 30, 90

of printed word, 10, 24, 28, 54, 220

of spoken word, 10, 24, 28, 35, 36, 54, 220

of story, 81, 83-4

Success, feeling of, 12, 37, 54, 55, 89, 154, 156, 191, 221, 222; *see also* Confidence

Suffixes, 117-18, 119

Syllabication, 117-24

Test results, 178, 179, 180, 181; *see also* Gates Primary Reading Tests

Tests; *see* Gates Primary Reading; Iowa; New York Tests of Growth in Reading

Thinking, 13, 22, 30, 31, 37, 59, 60

Thorndike, Edward L., 4

Tools, 10, 32, 35, 179, 211

Transfer, 5, 6, 22, 31, 36, 67, 75, 91, 92, 97, 98, 100, 156, 221

Visual discrimination; *see* Discrimination

Vocabulary

broadening of, 44, 84, 86-7, 103, 220

controlled, 35, 87

reading, 36, 37, 56, 66, 87, 88, 102, 105, 221

speaking, 42, 44, 47, 56, 91, 105, 153, 160

writing, 33, 36, 54, 60, 61, 90, 91, 95, 102, 105, 221; *see also* Sight vocabulary; Spelling; Writing

Vowels, 47, 54, 57, 63, 170, 177; *see also* Diphthongs

Wertheimer, Max, 5, 6, 10

Witty, Paul A., 36

Word attack, 8, 22, 26, 35, 179; *see also* Words, parts of; Sounding out

Word calling, 9, 64, 67

Word parts, function of, 12

Word recognition, 20, 26, 32, 35

clues to, 8, 19-21; *see also* Context; Key picture; Phonics approach; Words, shape of

Words

monosyllabic, 29, 33, 34, 35, 54, 57, 94, 117

parts of, 5, 10, 30, 34, 35, 57, 59, 62, 97, 98, 167, 168

phonetically irregular, 35, 105

phonetically regular, 30, 90, 91

role of, 33, 69, 77, 125, 198

shape of, 9, 10, 11, 12, 17, 19, 21, 26, 51

spoken, 10, 12, 22, 24, 29, 35, 36, 45, 56, 72; *see also* Structure, of spoken word

Writing, 22, 29, 33, 45, 49, 54, 59, 60, 93, 141, 144, 162, 163, 201; *see also* Games

Written record, 61, 74, 153